F

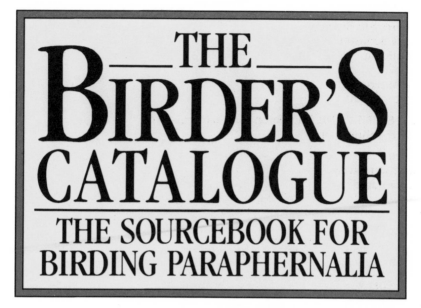

THE BIRDER'S CATALOGUE

THE SOURCEBOOK FOR BIRDING PARAPHERNALIA

By Sheila Buff

A Fireside Book
Published by Simon & Schuster Inc.
New York   London   Toronto   Sydney   Tokyo

A RUNNING HEADS BOOK

Simon and Schuster/Fireside Books,
Published by Simon & Schuster Inc.
Simon & Schuster Building
Rockefeller Center
1230 Avenue of the Americas
New York, New York   10020

SIMON AND SCHUSTER, FIRESIDE, and colophons are registered
trademarks of Simon & Schuster Inc.

The Birder's Catalogue
was conceived and produced by
Running Heads Incorporated,
42 East 23 Street
New York, New York   10010

Editor: Sarah Kirshner
Designer: Jack Tom

10 9 8 7 6 5 4 3 2 1
10 9 8 7 6 5 4 3 2 1 Pbk.

Library of Congress Cataloging in Publication Data

Buff, Sheila.
    The birder's catalogue.
    1. Bird watching.   2. Bird watching—Equipment and
supplies.   3. Bird watching—Societies, etc.
4. Birds, Protection of—Societies, etc.   I. Title.
QL677.5.B79   1988   598'.07'234   88-23917
·ISBN 0-671-66791-2
ISBN 0-671-66792-0 (pbk.)

Typeset by David E. Seham Associates Inc.
Color Separations by Hong Kong Scanner Craft Company Ltd.
Printed and bound in Singapore.

Every effort has been made to provide complete, accurate and up-to-
date information in this book. However, the world of bird lovers is
large and changeable, and there are doubtless some omissions and
errors. Suggestions, corrections and additions for future editions of
The Birder's Catalogue are welcome. Send to:
    The Birder's Catalogue
    Running Heads
    42 East 23 Street
    New York, NY   10010

In this book the names of organizations, companies and individuals
and the services and products they supply are given for information
only. Their inclusion does not imply an endorsement or recommen-
dation of any sort from the author, packager or publisher.

For Joe and Dagmar.

The many bird lovers I corresponded with and spoke to while writing this book were unfailingly friendly and helpful. I thank them all for their assistance, particularly: Dr. Bill Hardy of Holbrook Travel, Christine Indoe of the National Audubon Society, Eileen Schlagenhaft of Duncraft, and Jill Crane, Steven C. Sibley and Scott Sutcliffe of the Cornell Laboratory of Ornithology.

The work of writing this book was considerably leavened by the unfailing cheerfulness of Sarah Kirshner and her colleagues at Running Heads. Jack Tom's beautiful design brings the book to life. Finally, the support of Caroline Herter and Laura Yorke at Simon & Schuster helped make this project a success.

CONTENTS

1
WATCHING THE BIRDS

How to Know the Birds • Keeping Records • Bird Sounds • The Urban Birdwatcher • Cold-Weather Birding • Birding Gear • Other Outdoor Gear • Binoculars • Spotting Scopes • Where to Buy Optics • Cameras and Lenses • Tripods

HOW TO KNOW THE BIRDS

Anyone, even someone not at all interested in birds, can easily recognize a number of birds, at least in a general sort of way. Gulls, ducks, swans, geese, pigeons, sparrows, chickadees, crows, robins, mockingbirds, blue jays, cardinals, starlings, eagles, hawks, owls, penguins, vultures, parrots, parakeets, canaries, and more are all familiar, if not from the backyard and park then from visits to the zoo, books, television, magazines and movies.

If the average uninterested person can recognize twenty birds without really caring, someone who makes an interested effort can easily learn to recognize many more. If you make that effort, your rewards are far greater than just a list of birds. You will enter the marvelous, mysterious natural world and come to appreciate its beauties and complexities. You will learn about the delicate balance of nature and how easily it can be disrupted, and you will start to care passionately about preserving that balance.

Birdwatching is a sport for everyone. It can be as simple as scattering breadcrumbs on the grass and as complex as an expedition to the Antarctic. Adolescents can be enthusiastic and indefatigable birders; so can great-grandmothers.

To get started in birdwatching, two things are required: A good field guide (see pages 82–83) and good pair of binoculars—the very best you can afford. (See pages 18–20 for more on binoculars.)

Once in possession of these, you are ready to get serious about birds. First, *read* the field guide. Grasp the concept of bird families and learn the basic characteristics of each. For example, consider the family Paridae, commonly called titmice. These birds are small, plump and acrobatic, have small bills and usually are found in small groups. Within each family of birds are a number of species. For example, within the tit-

Catbirds are gray all over with a black cap. Their call sounds very much like a cat mewing.

Only the male painted bunting, a type of finch, is this colorful. Females are yellow-green all over.

4

Puffins in the Bay of Fundy, New Brunswick.

The familiar Canada goose is often found in parks and on golf courses.

mice family there are sixty-four species worldwide and four in eastern America. To determine the species of a bird, birders use identifying characteristics known as field marks. These are such things as bill type, color, shape and markings. Sometimes a single characteristic is sufficient to make a positive identification, but more often a combination of characteristics is needed. Thus, if you live in the east and a small, plump, acrobatic bird with a small bill appears at your feeder, you will know it is of the titmice family. Noting its black cap, white cheeks and the white streak on each wing, you will know from the titmice section of your field guide that it is a black-capped chickadee.

To complicate identifications, the male, female and juvenile birds of many species have different plumages. In addition, some birds have different winter and summer plumages.

Other important characteristics for identifying a bird include its size, behavior, flight characteristics, posture and so on. For example, a small brown bird with a slender bill creeping in a spiral up a tree trunk is a brown creeper, a close relative of nuthatches.

The overall impression of a bird— a combination of field marks, shape, behavior and an indefinable something—is what birders call "jizz." Examples of jizz are the jaunty angle of a mockingbird's tail, or the stealthy way a red-eyed vireo moves through the treetops. It is a grasp of a bird's jizz that lets an experienced birdwatcher recognize a bird at a single casual glance; a grasp of jizz is in turn the product of long experience and intuition.

The sounds a bird makes are an important clue to identifying it. Field guides attempt to give syllabic descriptions of bird songs, but there is no substitute for actually hearing the song. The best way is to go out into the field with someone who knows the songs and can identify them for you. The next best way is to listen to recordings (see page 87). Amplifying microphones with headsets that

Brown thrashers are in the same family as mockingbirds and catbirds.

can be carried into the field are sometimes useful for picking up faint calls (see page 11).

Bird identification becomes simpler if you take it gradually and logically rather than trying to memorize every bird in the field guide. If you are planning a field trip to a marsh in the summer, for example, prepare for it by looking up those birds you are likely to see. Since most birds have very specific ranges and ecological niches, you will be able to predict which birds will probably be there and thus have an easier time identifying them. During migration periods, when birds of all sorts may be passing through, this system will be less helpful. In fact, there may be so many new and different birds appearing

that you will be overwhelmed. This is a good time to join your local bird club or National Audubon Society chapter. Go on the field trips and bird walks and take advantage of the leader's expertise. One productive field trip in the company of an experienced birder is worth many hours of poring over a field guide. (For more information on bird organizations, see pages 64–77.)

An important part of birdwatching is identifying what you see and hear. Remember the words of Walt Whitman: "You must not know too much, or be too precise or scientific about birds and trees and flowers . . . ; a certain free margin, and even vagueness . . . helps your enjoyment of these things."

KEEPING RECORDS

Some casual birdwatchers never take any notes or keep any records of their activities. Most birdwatchers like to keep lists, however, and even lists of lists, and most take notes of their field observations. Lists provide a permanent record of your sightings and are a good way to refresh your memory and make interesting comparisons.

Checklists. Many bird sanctuaries, parks and wildlife refuges provide checklists of the birds known to have been found in the area; state and local checklists are often available from the state fish and game department and from local bird organizations. Checklists have a space to note the date, time, location and weather. The bird listings are organized by family and species. There is usually information about the status of each bird in the area, indicating whether the bird is a seasonal or permanent resident, if it breeds there, how common or rare it is, and so on. There is always a space for a check mark and sometimes there is space for comments. Checklists are a useful record of field trips and are the basis for forming life lists—never discard them.

Life lists. Your life list is just that: a record of all the birds you have seen to date. There are numerous ways to keep your life list. Some people simply make check marks, while others keep detailed records. A life bird or "lifer" is a species seen for the first time in a birdwatcher's career in the sport.

Other lists. Many feeder watchers keep monthly (or more frequent) lists of the birds that come to eat. Birders also keep lists of all the birds seen on a single day (a Christmas bird count, January 1 or fall migration day, for example), all the birds seen in a single location, all the breeding birds seen and almost any other imaginable combination.

Notebooks. A notebook of a convenient size is the next most important tool after your field guide and binoculars. Different people have different preferences in notebooks. Some purchase expensive, bound notebooks with waterproof covers, while others prefer the sort of cheap, spiralbound notebook that can be bought in supermarkets. Since your notebook will certainly get rained on, dropped in puddles and dunked in streams, waterproofing makes a certain amount of sense. Also because your notebook will get wet, use a pencil or ballpoint pen; anything else will run and blur. Whichever writing implement you choose, be sure it is inexpensive and carry several, since they tend to get lost. Into your notebook go remarks on the season, weather, habitat and location, listings of the species you see, sketches and notes about unidentified birds, observations about appearance, behavior and field marks, notes on flora and fauna, directions, phone numbers and other odds and ends. Your water-stained, muddy, torn notebooks contain your birding life; treasure them.

A B C	Species	North Florida Months	North Florida Abundance	South Florida Months	South Florida Abundance
	Phalacrocoracidae—Cormorants				
	Great Cormorant	10-4	o	11-6	o
	Double-crested Cormorant*	R	c-a	R	c-a
	Anhingidae—Darters				
	Anhinga*	R	o-c	R	u-a
	Fregatidae—Frigatebirds				
	Magnificent Frigatebird*	4-12	o-u	R	o-a
	Ardeidae—Bitterns and Herons				
	American Bittern*	8-5+	o-u	8-5+	o-r
	Least Bittern*	3-11+	o-u	R	o-fc
	Great Blue Heron (incl. Great White Heron)*	R	fc-c	R	u-a
	Great Egret*	R	fc-a	R	fc-a
	Snowy Egret*	R	o-c	R	fc-a
	Little Blue Heron*	R	fc-c	R	fc-a
	Tricolored Heron*	R	o-c	R	u-a
	Reddish Egret*	R	o-u	R	o-fc
	Cattle Egret*	2-11+	fc-a	R	a
	Green-backed Heron*	3-10+	u-c	R	fc-c
	Black-crowned Night-Heron*	R	o-fc	R	o-c
	Yellow-crowned Night-Heron*	3-10+	o-u	R	o-c
	Threskiornithidae—Ibis and Spoonbills				
	White Ibis*	R	u-a	R	fc-a
	Scarlet Ibis (incl. presumed hybrids)*	6	o	R	o
	Glossy Ibis*	R	o-a	R	o-a
	White-faced Ibis*	3-5	o	6	o
	Roseate Spoonbill*	4-10+	o-r	R	o-c
	Ciconiidae—Storks				
	Wood Stork*	3-12+	o-c	R	o-a
	Phoenicopteridae—Flamingos				
	Greater Flamingo	3-10	o	R	local

A red-bellied woodpecker searches for insects. Note the red head and striped back; the belly is actually white.

Meadowlarks are found in grassy country. The eastern and western species are very similar.

The song of the rufous-sided towhee is "drink your tea!"

A nest of robin's eggs. Robins usually raise two broods in a season.

Smaller than common pigeons, mourning doves have a pointed tail edged with white spots.

BIRD SOUNDS

Birds can be attracted in the field by imitating their sounds. Some people have a natural talent for this and are able to whistle convincing renditions of bird songs. Less talented birders must resort to bird callers that make squeaking and whistling sounds. Another method is to make squeaks by smacking the lips against the back of the hand. A technique known as pishing is also quite effective, although no one really knows why. It involves making rhythmic hissing noises that apparently mimic the distress calls of some birds; on the other hand, maybe the birds respond simply because they are curious. This interesting procedure is not for everyone, as Christopher Leahy points out in his delightful and informative book *The Birdwatcher's Companion:* "Like peering with an (apparently) vacant expression into the air or wading about in fetid marshland, pishing may direct a certain amount of not altogether approving human attention to the birdwatcher. But the effect of the technique depends on a certain emotional commitment and unembarrassed vigor, and fainthearted birders will do as well to remain silent."

Recording the birds. Really serious birders can invest large sums of money in parabolic microphones and complex tape recorders and make their own recordings of bird songs. As long as the recording is done in a way that has no harmful effect on the birds or environment, this is an interesting aspect of the sport that has genuine scientific value, since researchers are only starting to understand the full meaning of bird noises. Ethical questions can arise when the songs are played back as a means of attracting birds, however. Within limits the birds simply respond as they would to a bird caller. But taking it to the point where the birds think other birds are invading their territory, for example, is definitely going beyond the limits of proper birding behavior.

Learning to watch birds in an ornithology class in Maine.

Watching ospreys in Florida with guide Flip Pallott.

Birdwatching with Flip Pallott from a canoe in Florida. This is often the best way to see birds in swampy areas.

Eavesdropping on the Birds

Amplifying microphones attached to earphones are sometimes, but not always, a helpful way to hear the sounds of distant birds. Compact, battery-powered units are available from several manufacturers.

BPA Marketing
3519 Bigelow Boulevard
Pittsburgh, PA 15213

Jason Empire
9200 Cody
Overland Park, KS 66214

Silver Creek Industries
1909 Silver Creek Road
Manitowoc, WI 54221

The opposite of jungle birding is Antarctic birding, here with Society Expeditions.

Jungle birding on a Society Expeditions trip.

This song sparrow is perched at the top of a tree, singing to indicate its territory.

Birding in the spring woods. Note the shoulder stock mount for the spotting scope this birdwatcher carries.

THE URBAN BIRDWATCHER

A common misconception about cities is that they are concrete jungles where a few of the most ordinary birds—pigeons, house sparrows, starlings—are ubiquitous and other birds nonexistent. This is simply not so. Even among the concrete canyons of dense urban concentrations fascinating and varied bird life can be found, if you know where and how to look.

New York City, for example, is often thought of as the epitome of bird-free urbanization, yet this is far from true. The Jamaica Bay Wildlife Refuge, part of the Gateway National Recreation Area, is literally in the shadow of Kennedy Airport, yet more than 300 bird species have been seen there. Central Park, an 800-acre (320-ha) haven in the heart of skyscraper Manhattan, is a paradise for birders in the migration seasons, and more than 250 species have been sighted there. Birding walks in the 33-acre (13-ha) section of the park known as the Ramble can be very rewarding.

Every city has parks and open areas that will be fruitful places to look for birds. Often there are enjoyable birding areas in parks and open areas only a few miles beyond the city limits. Every state has chapters of the National Audubon Society; most cities have a local chapter or a nature club that sponsors field trips, bird walks, lectures and more. These activities are usually free or have only a nominal cost. They are often listed in local papers and in calendars of community events. Once you start to look for the announcements, you may be surprised at how many there are. You may also be pleasantly surprised at how friendly everyone is and at how much of nature can be seen in your city, if only you look.

Feeding the birds in a city has a few twists. It's one thing to toss a pizza crust into a flock of pigeons. It's another thing altogether to attract desirable birds to a city feeder. Be realistic. You will not have much success if your feeder is above the fifth floor. You need to have access to some open space—a vacant lot, roof garden, patio, backyard or park. Unfortunately, the smaller the space the harder it is to keep squirrels—especially wily urban squirrels—away. Select a feeder that is as squirrel-proof as possible. Another urban problem is the stray cat population. Eternal vigilance is the only answer. To keep pigeons out of the feeder, avoid the table and tray kinds. Stick with hanging or post-mounted tube or ball feeders equipped with squirrel baffles. Brackets that hold hanging feeders and are designed to attach to balcony railings or window sills may be useful for people without yards but with second-floor terraces or windows. Keep the area under the feeder clean. Spilled seeds will attract unwanted vermin like mice and rats. If you notice rats around the feeder area, clean the area and stop feeding until the rats go away.

Urban birds often have a difficult time finding water. Putting out a birdbath

Birding On Line

Some birdwatchers keep their life lists on index cards in an old shoe box. Others have gone high tech and keep their lists on computer disks. Listing software that allows you to manipulate and analyze your data is available.

Birdlist
Bird Commander, Inc.
Box 34238
Bethesda, MD 20817
(301) 229-7002

This program needs an IBM PC-compatible computer with a 128K memory. It allows you to create and maintain detailed life and annual lists for the United States and Canada along with five discretionary lists. The program contains a built-in data base of all North American and Hawaiian birds; the information can be used to print out target lists for the birds you still need to see. An optional subscription to a quarterly update helps keep the data base current. The program was created by Tony White, an experienced trip leader whose North American life list contains over 600 species seen over 30 years; his articles have appeared in *Birding* magazine.

BirdBase
World Bird Base
Santa Barbara Software Products
1400 Dover Road
Santa Barbara, CA 93103
(805) 963-4886

This program runs on IBM PC-compatible computers with a minimum memory of 192K. The system allows for up-to-date versions of your inclusive life list and eight specialized life lists; any entry to one life list can be automatically recorded on the others as desired. The program also features a rapid double-index system for sorting bird sightings. The data base of bird species includes all birds of the continental United States and Canada; up to 500 accidentals and/or birds from other regions can be added. The data base can be used to create target and specialized lists.

World Birdbase is designed for use by serious birdwatchers and professional naturalists. The database includes the scientific and common names of the world's 9,200 birds. The program runs on IBM-compatible PCs with hard disk memories; the data can be output to disk files.

BIRDS (Bird Information and Retrieval Data System)
Scientia Enterprises
2536 Cedar Canyon Drive
Marietta, GA 30067

This program runs on IBM PC-compatible computers with a minimum memory of 128K. DOS 2.1 and BASIC are also required. The program allows you to create seasonal or area checklists, maintain several types of life lists, create target lists and more. It also has an historical summary spread sheet and a master file maintenance subsystem.

(raised to reduce the danger from cats) and keeping it filled with clean water is likely to attract more birds than the feeder will.

In some cities it is illegal to feed pigeons; also, you may be forbidden to feed birds by the terms of your lease. Be sure your feeding of the birds does not go beyond the law.

The more urban your neighborhood the less likely you are to attract interesting birds, but it is still worth the effort. Blue jays, cardinals, chickadees, robins, dark-eyed juncos, mockingbirds, mourning doves, flickers and other birds are often found in urban areas. And if you provide food and water during the migration periods, some interesting visitors will probably make brief stops. Even if you don't attract a lot of garden birds, make the best of what you do attract. By watching the activities of house sparrows, for example, you will learn quite a bit about bird behavior in general and you will be practicing your observation skills as well. You'll find that these cheerful if maligned little birds are really quite amusing. Even pigeons can be interesting, since no two have exactly the same markings.

Urban Raptors

As the success of rock doves (better known as pigeons) proves, for some birds there's not a lot of difference between natural cliffs and tall buildings. In 1977, a young female peregrine falcon was released by The Peregrine Fund at a wildlife refuge near the mouth of northeastern Maryland's Gunpowder River. Shortly thereafter, she was spotted in Baltimore on and around the thirty-seven-story USF&G Insurance building, the highest "cliff" in the city. She chose to nest on the south ledge of the thirty-third floor. With no lack of pigeons to support her, Scarlett, as the employees named her, was content to stay. The next step for The Peregrine Fund and USF&G was to help Scarlett raise a family. In 1979 she failed to form a pair bond

Blythe and her eyases on a ledge of the USF&G Building.

with either of two male candidates introduced for that purpose and laid three infertile eggs. At the proper time, scientists introduced three young eyases (falcon chicks) hatched in the lab, which Scarlett raised. In 1980 a male named Rhett was introduced, and pair bonding resulted, although the eggs were again infertile. Again, laboratory-born eyases were substituted, and Scarlett adopted and raised all five. Two more males, Percy and Ashley, were introduced in 1982 and 1983. Percy didn't like city living, but Ashley adapted. Once again, the eggs were infertile, and eyases were substituted. Astonishingly, in 1983 a wild male peregrine, dubbed Beauregard, found his way to Scarlett. The two mated successfully and raised a brood of four. In 1984 Scarlett died at the age of seven, having raised twenty-one eyases in all. The saddened Beauregard was soon consoled by the natural arrival of a wild female falcon, who was named Blythe. The two have been producing healthy young since 1985.

COLD-WEATHER BIRDING

Birdwatching in cold weather can range from sitting comfortably indoors admiring the visitors at the window feeder all the way to Arctic expeditions. Those serious enough to travel to Attu, Alaska, for instance, to watch the spring migration probably are sufficiently informed about the necessary gear and precautions. However, every year many less experienced birdwatchers participate in winter field trips, Christmas bird counts and other outdoor activities that can lead to hypothermia or frostbite if precautions are not taken.

Hypothermia. A drop in body temperature of more than 4°F (2°C) can lead to the dangerous and possibly fatal condition known as hypothermia. Prolonged exposure to cold and windy weather, especially if you are improperly dressed, is a good way to bring on hypothermia; so is getting wet, even if you are properly dressed. Healthy young people are less susceptible than children and the elderly. Symptoms include uncontrollable shivering, mental confusion, lethargy, clumsiness, irritability and slurred speech. Death can result if the victim is not promptly treated. Because the symptoms develop gradually as the victim gets colder, they may not be noticed until too late. You will probably not notice them in yourself, so never go out in extremely cold conditions alone.

To prevent hypothermia, *dress appropriately for the weather.* This means

The vest from Lepp and Associates.

several layers of warm clothing under a wind- and waterproof outer layer. Wear warm gloves, proper footwear and a warm hat that covers the ears. Do not drink alcohol.

To treat hypothermia, get the victim to a warm, or at least sheltered, place as soon as possible. Replace any wet clothing with dry. If the victim is conscious and not likely to choke, give him warm, nonalcoholic drinks. Hypothermia is a serious condition—get medical help after taking the first aid steps.

Frostbite means that the skin and tissues beneath the skin have frozen. It is a serious medical problem that requires prompt attention. Frostbitten skin is pale and hard; it has no feeling. Your ears, hands, nose and feet are most likely to become frostbitten. Should this happen, the affected part should be gradually warmed. Get indoors if possible, or at least out of the wind if not. Cover the frozen part with blankets or clothing, or warm it against your body (by tucking the hands into the armpits, for example), or place it in warm water at about 100°F (38°C). Never rub snow against the affected part; in fact, never the rub the area at all, and never apply direct heat. When the frostbitten parts begin to warm up, they may be red and tender. Move the parts gently as they warm. However, do not walk on frostbitten feet. Frostbite is a serious condition—get medical help after taking the first aid steps.

Tamrac makes a roomy photographer's vest.

The Birder's Buddy vest in action.

BIRDING GEAR
Birding Vests

Birders like comfortable, efficient clothing with lots of pockets, which are needed to hold the field guides, notebooks, checklists, pencils, film cans, camera lenses, handkerchiefs, oranges, sandwiches, hats, canteens, bird callers and other essential paraphernalia a birdwatcher needs. Birding vests are a good way to get some extra pockets. These lightweight, sturdy vests have much in common with the vests designed for photographers. They are made by several manufacturers.

Birder's Buddy
330 South Ash Lane
Flagstaff, AZ 86004

Columbia Sportswear Company
6600 North Baltimore
Portland, OR 97203

Helix Company
310 South Racine Avenue
Chicago, IL 60607

OTHER OUTDOOR GEAR

The gear birders need—parkas, hiking boots, backpacks—is much the same as that needed by any outdoors lover. The suppliers listed below offer mail-order catalogs of camping and hiking clothing and equipment.

Banana Republic
Box 7737
San Francisco, CA 94120
(800) 772-9977

L.L. Bean, Inc.
Freeport, ME 04033
(800) 221-4221

Cabela's
Sidney, NE 69160
(308) 254-5505

Patagonia
Box 86
230 South Olive Street
Ventura, CA 93002
(805) 648-3386

Ramsey Outdoor, Inc.
226 Route 17
Paramus, NJ 07652
(201) 261-5000

REI
Box 88127
Seattle, WA 98138
(800) 426-4840

Campmor
Box 998
Paramus, NJ 07653
(201) 445-5000

Birding for Everyone

Birdwatching is a sport that can give pleasure to all, regardless of age or physical ability. Many elderly people are devoted feeder watchers who also enjoy nonstrenuous bird walks. Nearly all federal and state parks now have facilities for the physically handicapped. In many cases the nature walks in the park are fully or partially accessible.

Birdwatching is as much listening as watching. Because of this, many visually handicapped people enjoy birds. An excellent booklet called *Birding: An Introduction to Ornithological Delights for Blind and Physically Handicapped Individuals* is available from the Library of Congress. The booklet contains a list of the many recordings of books about birds available through the library at no charge, as well as other information. For a free copy, call (202) 287-5100 or write to:

Birding
CMLS
Box 9150
Melbourne, FL 32902

BINOCULARS

A good pair of binoculars is probably the single most important investment a serious birder can make. There are a number of factors to consider when making your choice. Price is one, of course, but a higher price does not necessarily mean a better pair of binoculars. On the other hand, it may well be worthwhile to spend a little more and get a pair of binoculars that you will be happy with for a long time—and good binoculars can last a lifetime. As with any expensive purchase, be informed and shop around. To help, below are short explanations of the important concepts and technical terms.

Magnification. Binoculars are often described by their magnification and lens diameter; for example, 7 × 50. The first number in this equation indicates the magnification. Thus binoculars that magnify seven times (7x) will make objects appear to be seven times closer—that is, a bird that is 70 feet away will appear to be only 10 feet away when seen through the binoculars.

Lens diameter. The second number in the description 7 × 50 indicates the diameter of the lens (also called the objective) in millimeters (multiply by 0.04 for the equivalent in inches). Since bigger objectives gather more light, the larger the lens the brighter the image and the better you can see in dim light.

Exit pupil. If a pair of binoculars is held up to a light, a circle of light is seen in the eyepiece. This circle is known as the exit pupil. Optimally, its diameter should match the maximum size the pupil of your eye can dilate to under the lighting conditions you are most likely to encounter. Under very dim conditions the eye's pupil can dilate to a diameter no wider than one-quarter of an inch (7mm). Thus binoculars that would be useful for observations in early dawn or twilight conditions would have an exit pupil of about one-quarter of an inch (7mm); with an exit pupil of only

The Swift Audubon binoculars have an extra-wide field of view and are a superior choice for the serious birder.

2/16 inch (4mm) or 3/16 inch (5mm), the binoculars would be useful only in full daylight. However, the eye's ability to dilate decreases with age. For middle-aged and older people, binoculars with an exit pupil of more than 3/16 inch (5mm) are a waste, since some of the light coming through the eyepiece would fall outside the pupil of the eye and not be perceived. The exit pupil number is not marked on the binoculars. Ask the salesperson or check the descriptive literature provided by the manufacturer.

Relative brightness index (RBI). To determine the relative brightness index, simply square the exit pupil size. This is not really a very useful number for comparing brightness between binoculars, but it is one that is often used by manufacturers.

Twilight factor. The twilight factor is a more useful relative measure of brightness, especially for birders who will be observing under less than full daylight conditions. It measures viewing efficiency and image detail in twilight conditions. To calculate the factor (if it is not in the manufacturer's literature), multiply the magnification by the diameter of the objective, and then find the square root of the product. The larger the factor, the more efficient the binoculars are in dim light. For example, 8 × 32 binoculars would have a twilight factor of 16, while 20 × 80 binoculars would have a twilight factor of 40. The 20 × 80 binoculars would thus be better for dim light conditions, even though both might have the same exit pupils. For dim light, a twilight factor of at least 20 is recommended.

Prisms. All binoculars use prisms to orient the image correctly; otherwise,

Endorsed by the National Audubon Society, the Bushnell 7 × 35 binoculars are a good choice for any birder.

you would see things upside-down through the binoculars. The quality of the prism has a great effect on the quality of the image. To determine the quality of the prism, hold the binoculars up to light and look at the exit pupil. In the best binoculars the exit pupils are perfect circles. Lesser quality prisms produce exit pupils that have gray areas cutting across the edges, making them look like square pegs in round holes. The result is that the image in the vignetted area is much too dim or even totally cut off.

Near focus. The closest distance at which the binoculars can focus is called near focus. For a pair of 7×50 binoculars, this would be about 18 to 20 feet. Generally, the more powerful the binoculars the larger the near focus distance.

Coatings. As light passes through the various optical elements that make up a pair of binoculars, it can be reflected back, leading to fuzzy, hazy and dim images. By coating the elements with extremely thin layers of magnesium fluoride, the reflection problem is considerably reduced. To check the quality of the coatings, look at the color of the light reflected from them. Coatings done correctly will generally appear purple-violet, although the color can range from pale blue to blue-magenta. If the coating is too thin it will appear pink; if it is too thick, it will appear green. Multi-coatings are generally green, although the color can vary depending on the type of coatings. Beware: some cheap binoculars are coated only on the front of the objective lens and the rear of the eyepiece to give the impression that all elements are coated.

Field of view. The size, expressed in degrees (angular field) or feet or meters (linear field), of the area you can see through a pair of binoculars is called the field of view. In either case, the larger the field of view the larger the area that appears in the image. Wide field of view is useful when observing things, like birds or sports, that are likely

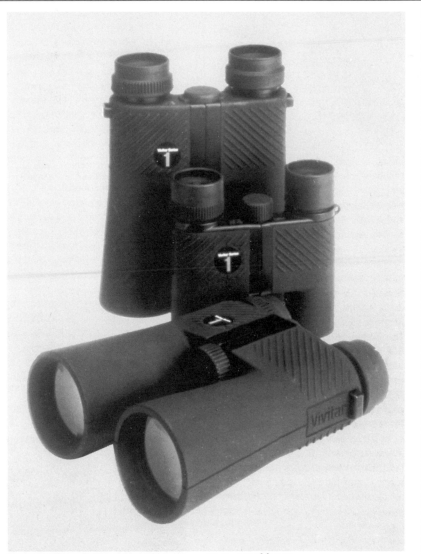

Binoculars from Vivitar offer several choices of fully coated lenses.

to move; the narrower the field of view, the more often you will have to move and refocus the binoculars to keep the subject in view. Field of view is relative to magnification. The greater the magnification, the smaller the field of view usually is. Field of view is usually indicated on the body of the binoculars in degrees, feet and meters. For example, the marking "410 ft at 1000 yds" indicates that at 1,000 yards the field of view is 410 feet wide.

Collimation. The technical term for the alignment of optical elements is collimation. Improper collimation, most often caused by misaligned prisms, will result in poor images: ghost images, distortion and color fringing (rainbowing). Viewers may develop headaches and eyestrain after a long session with poorly aligned binoculars.

Eye relief. The distance between the end of the eyepiece (the part that is held to the eye) and the actual lens is called the eye relief. The distance can vary between models and from manufacturer

Swift Osprey binoculars weigh only 28 ounces and are very good for the field.

to manufacturer. A longer distance is thought to be more comfortable for eyeglass wearers and for extended use, but some feel the degree of eye relief is a matter of personal preference.

Body styles. Binoculars are available in three basic body types: the German Z (Zeiss), the American B (Bushnell) and the roof-prism H. Types Z and B use porro prisms (two triangular prisms offset from each other). This allows the objectives to be larger. Type H uses two roof-shaped prisms placed one behind the other. This allows H-type binoculars to be lighter and more compact, but the objectives cannot be as large. Z-type binoculars have separate front barrels screwed into the body; this is cheaper to manufacture and align, but it does mean more places where moisture can

H-type binoculars from Swarovski Optik are waterproof and especially good for wet field conditions.

get in. B-type binoculars have a body that is basically one piece and thus somewhat sturdier. H-type binoculars are also one-piece, but because the roof-prism arrangement is harder to make and align, they are more expensive.

Accessories. Generally the purchase price of the binoculars includes a neck strap, carrying case and lens caps. Tripod adapters allow the binoculars to be mounted on a standard tripod for more stable, vibration-free viewing.

When choosing binoculars, it is always a good idea to select the rubber-coated version. These binoculars won't make noise when they knock against a canteen, for example, and are more likely to survive an accidental dunking. Another feature to look for is a central focusing knob, which focuses the binoculars using a single knurled wheel; adjustments to differences between the eyes are made using the adjustable right eyepiece. Individual focusing binoculars, which are adjusted to each eye, are very sturdy (in part because they are built to military specifications), but they are not particularly convenient to use. Fast-focus levers are sometimes useful, but

they are restricted by mechanical considerations to the less-expensive models. Soft rubber eyecups are useful for blocking out distracting light; they also make viewing more comfortable for those who wear eyeglasses. Other factors to consider are weight and balance, but the only criteria here is what feels comfortable to the individual.

Using Binoculars

Interpupillary distance. The distance between the eyes varies from person to person. Look through the binoculars and move the two halves until you see one clear circle of image.

Focus. To focus central-focus binoculars, first close the right eye and look through the left side with the left eye. Rotate the focusing knob until the image is sharp. Next, close the left eye and look through the right side with the right eye. Rotate the right eyepiece until the image is sharp. For the rest of the viewing session use just the center focus knob to refocus.

CAUTION! Never look at the sun through binoculars! Serious eye damage can result.

The Leupold 20 × 60 spotting scope is compact, lightweight, rugged and waterproof.

SPOTTING SCOPES

Spotting scopes are basically compact telescopes. They are particularly useful for long-distance observations from a fixed vantage point; for example, observing an eagle's nest. In addition, by adding a camera adapter, spotting scopes can be used as telephoto lenses for photography.

A good spotting scope can be a major investment of nearly a thousand dollars and potentially much more. Much of the terminology used to describe spotting scopes, such as exit pupil and twilight factor. is the same as that for binoculars (see pages 18–20).

Scope Types

Spotting scopes come in two types: refractor (prismatic) or catadioptric (lens/mirror).

Refractor scopes. Designed for wide-angle, low-magnification viewing of fairly close subjects, refractor scopes contain a built-in erecting prism to provide a correctly oriented image, which is why they are sometimes called prismatic. Most refractors come with zoom eyepieces ranging from 15x to 45x or 60x.

Catadioptric scopes. With a narrower field of view and greater magnification than refractor scopes, catadioptric scopes are excellent for observing distant subjects. These scopes use an arrangement of lenses and mirrors to "fold" a long optical path into a compact package. This allows for high magnification within a compact and relatively lightweight scope. Catadioptric scopes usually come with an eyepiece that shows the image right-side up but backward. However, some have erecting prisms, which show the image correctly, as standard equipment. Erecting prisms can be added to those scopes that do not have them. The eyepiece on a catadioptric scope usually has a fixed focal length; for greater magnification longer eyepieces can be added.

The Zoom Master II spotting scope from Celestron zooms from 15 to 60 power, a ratio of 4:1.

Celestron's affordable model C65 spotting scope is both lightweight and durable; it is designed for rugged use in the field.

The C90 is Celestron's most popular spotting scope. Weighing only 3 ½ pounds (1.6 kg) and measuring less than 8 inches (20 cm) in length, this versatile scope is beautifully made.

Scope Terminology

Focusing. Two types of focusing systems are used on spotting scopes. The helical system is a collar either around the barrel of the scope or on the eyepiece. Since only a turn or two is needed to focus, this system is best for following action. The micrometric system uses a knob at the rear of the scope. This system is more precise, but it requires many more turns to focus.

Near focus. The nearest distance the scope can be focused for close-up work is the near focus. The near focus for a refractor scope is generally about 25 feet (7.5m); for a catadioptric scope it is usually about 10 feet (3m).

F stop. Because catadioptric spotting scopes are often used as long photographic lenses, the f stop, or aperture diameter, is often indicated in the sales literature. Most are f/11, though some are a stop higher or lower.

Other factors. Spotting scopes are too heavy to hold steady by hand. Tripod adapters are built in, and a sturdy tripod is needed (see page 26). The purchase price usually includes the eyepiece, lens shade, lens cap and case; camera adapters are additional.

The 23 × 75 Swarovski Optik twin telescope is excellent for observation at great distances.

The Songscope 1 microphone/amplifier attaches to your binoculars.

WHERE TO BUY OPTICS

Most reliable camera stores carry binoculars, and the larger stores will also carry spotting scopes. Prices are usually somewhat below list (and negotiable) and the sales staff will be reasonably knowledgeable. Department stores also carry binoculars; those with very large camera departments may also carry spotting scopes. These stores will often advertise very attractive prices on binoculars. Be extremely wary—store-brand binoculars are unlikely to be good, and poor binoculars are simply a waste of money.

A good way to purchase high-quality optics is through an experienced and reliable mail-order house. The selection is wide and the prices are often well below list. Some sources are:

Ad-Libs Astronomics
2401 Tee Circle
Norman, OK 73069
(405) 364-0858

Birding
Box 5
Amsterdam, NY 12010
(518) 842-0863

Robert Manns and Associates
877 Glenbrook Drive
Atlanta, GA 30318
(404) 352-3579

Swan Optical Co.
Box 813217
Smyrna, GA 30081

Telescope Exchange
4347 Sepulveda Boulevard
Culver City, CA 90230
(213) 397-0871

For optical equipment and binocular and optical repair:

Mirakel Optical Co., Inc.
331 Mansion Street
West Coxsackie, NY 12192
(518) 731-2610

Redlich Binoculars & Optical
2319 Wilson Boulevard
Arlington, VA 22201
(703) 527-5151

For camera and lens repair:

Professional Camera Repair Service Inc.
37 West 47 Street
New York, NY 10036
(212) 382-0550

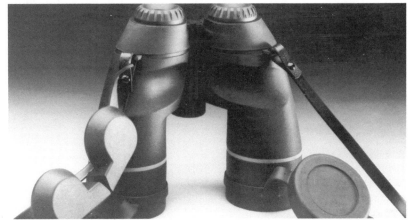

Swarovski Optik's sturdy, waterproof 10 × 50 binoculars come with attached lens caps that eliminate the need for a case.

The sound from the Jason Discovery sound amplifier is transmitted through the lightweight headphones.

These 8 × 32 Ultima binoculars from Celestron are an outstanding choice for the dedicated birder. The high quality of the optical elements contributes to the excellent image.

CAMERAS AND LENSES

For many, part of the joy of birdwatching is photographing birds. Almost all field photography today is done with lightweight and convenient 35mm cameras, usually of the automatic-exposure sort. These cameras are basically all similar in concept, although they can vary widely in features and in cost. For bird photography the basic camera requirements are straightforward: the camera must be rugged, it must accept long telephoto lenses and it must be quiet. When shopping for a camera, be sure to listen to it. All other factors being equal, choose the camera that makes the least noise when the shutter is tripped and the film is advanced, using either the lever or a built-in autowinder. Be sure that if the camera beeps or otherwise makes noises (when the exposure is checked, for example) the feature can be turned off.

Telephoto Lenses

The same considerations that go into buying any fine optical device apply when purchasing a telephoto lens. Any lens that is between 135mm and 1000mm in focal length is considered a telephoto, although most nature photography is done with a 400mm or 500mm lens. The basic choice is between standard lenses and catadioptric or mirror lenses. Although catadioptric lenses are lighter, smaller and often cheaper than standard telephotos, and also have less of the chromatic aberration found in very long telephotos, they have the serious disadvantage of a fixed aperture, usually at about f/8. To vary the exposure, the shutter speed or film speed must be varied. Standard telephoto lenses offer variable apertures, although the maximum aperture on a typical 400mm lens is f/4.5. Long lenses are also heavy—a tripod is a must. Zoom telephotos (200mm to 400mm, for example) offer increased flexibility with excellent optical quality; they are

far from cheap, however. An alternative to buying a very long lens is to purchase a shorter lens and a high-quality tele-extender matched to the lens. Available in 2x and 3x magnifications, these devices fit between the camera body and the lens and extend the focal length. For example, a 2x tele-extender used with a 300mm lens provides an effective focal length of 600mm. The drawback to tele-extenders is that they reduce the amount of light reaching the film by at least one or two f-stops.

No high-quality long telephoto lens is inexpensive. For about the same cost as a 600mm lens, a serious birder could purchase a good spotting scope with a camera adapter.

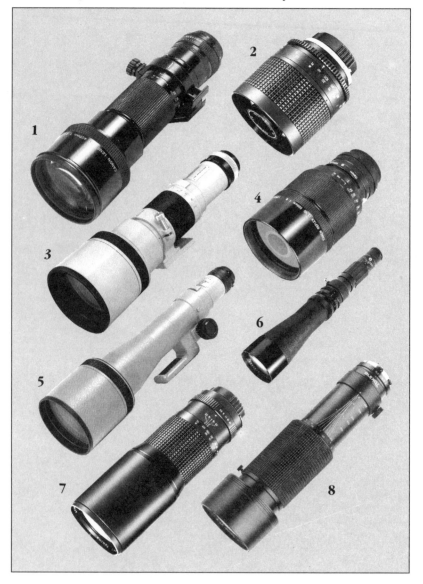

1.) A 400 mm standard lens from Canon. 2.) The catadioptric 500mm lens from Tokina is very compact. 3.) Canon's standard 500mm lens. 4.) Canon's catadioptric 500mm lens. 5.) The powerful 800mm lens from Canon. 6.) The 800mm lens from Tokina. 7.) Tokina makes a 400mm lens that opens up to f/5.6. 8.) 150-500mm zoom lens from Tokina

1.) With a maximum aperture of f/5.6, this 400mm lens from Sigma fits all manual-focus cameras. 2.) Lightweight and compact, this 600mm mirror (catadioptric) lens is from Sigma. 3.) This 100-500mm zoom lens is from Vivitar. 4.) Made by Sigma, this 100-500mm zoom lens has a maximum aperture of f/5.6 at 100mm and f/8 at 500mm. 5.) The 500mm APO lens from Sigma is designed for auto-focus cameras.

TRIPODS

For extended viewing through binoculars, and for any viewing with a spotting scope or telescope, a tripod is a necessity. Which tripod to choose depends on many considerations, but don't compromise. If you've just spent a small fortune to buy the binoculars or spotting scope of your dreams, get a good sturdy tripod to support it. Select one that is solid but lightweight, with as little wobble as possible. Center bracing helps. Many birders prefer flip-lock levers to adjust the legs of the tripod. The head (where the scope attaches to the tripod) should be simple to use. Ideally, one lever will control the head's horizontal and vertical movement, so viewing doesn't have to interrupted by fumbling to make adjustments. Fluid heads allow for smooth, even panning with little effort. A quick-release system on the head is desirable because it allows the binoculars to be attached and removed quickly and easily, even while wearing gloves.

Table-top tripods. Designed for use with spotting scopes, table-top tripods are compact, sturdy and rigid. They rarely rise more than 16 inches (40 cm), however, so their use is limited.

Car pods. Small but sturdy tripods that mount onto a car window or the like are very valuable. Because the tripod clamps onto a partially lowered window to provide a stable platform for viewing, it is very useful where it might be dangerous or unpleasant to leave the car—on a safari or when the weather is very severe, for example.

Shoulder mounts. There are times when a tripod is just inconvenient—too heavy to carry on a long hike, too awkward on a boat, or too slow to adjust for fast-moving birds. Shoulder mounts are a good option in these circumstances. The spotting scope is mounted onto a lightweight adjustable frame with a handgrip at the front and a shoulder stock at the rear. Shoulder mounts are usually available for binoculars.

From Bogen, three ways to support your optical gear: tripod, monopod and carpod.

26

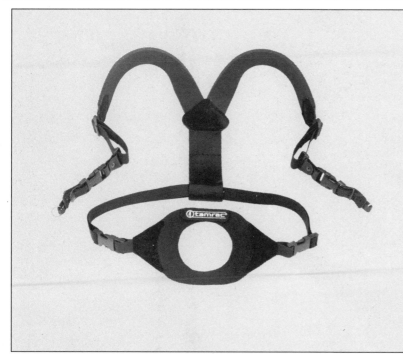

To hold your camera in place while you hike, try the Tamrac X-Press harness.

The Pro Harness can be used to hold binoculars or a camera.

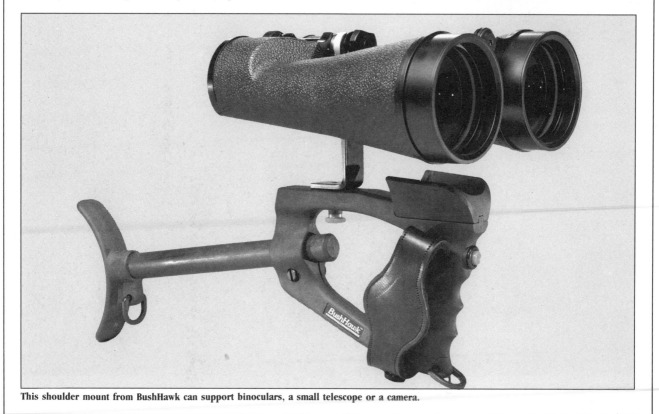

This shoulder mount from BushHawk can support binoculars, a small telescope or a camera.

Using the Bionic Ear from Silver Creek Industries, birders may hear birds at a greater distance. The system can also be used to make recordings.

The Bionic Booster, a parabolic microphone from Silver Creek Industries, increases the range of the Bionic Ear.

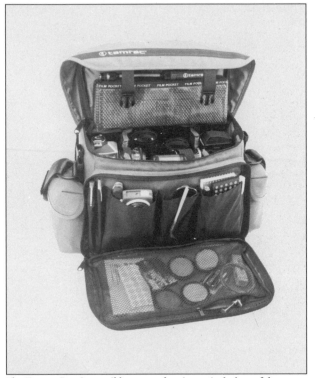

When on the trail, the Tamrac Photopack carries a lot and also allows quick and easy access to your gear.

The Tamrac Pro Convertible camera bag is particularly useful when traveling.

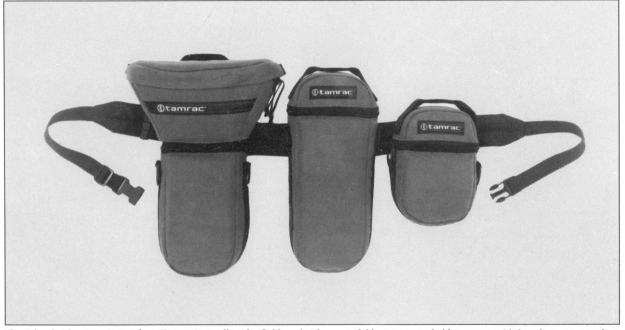

The Telepak Adventure System from Tamrac is excellent for field work. The expandable system can hold a camera with long lens, an extra lens and a gear pouch.

Optical Accessories
The companies listed below are good sources for assorted paraphernalia.

Lepp and Associates
Box 6240
Los Osos, CA 93412
(805) 528-7385
Blinds and other gear.

Tamrac
6709 Independence Avenue
Canoga Park, CA 91303
(818) 715-0090
Carrying cases for optical equipment.

Tripods and Other Supports
Bogen Photo
17-20 Willow Street
Fair Lawn, NJ 07410
(201) 794-6500

BushHawk
312 Banks Street
San Diego, CA 92110
(800) 325-8542/(619) 296-2240

Straps
ProHarness
Marlab Specialties
Box 4019
San Rafael, CA 94903
(800) 237-4293

Windsong Ministrap
Windsong Film Impressions
Box 201
Glendenen Beach, OR 97388
(503) 764-2972

Periodicals for Photographers
Outdoor Photographer
16000 Ventura Boulevard
Suite 800
Encino, CA 91436
(818) 986-8400
10 times/year; single issue $2.95,
    annual subscription $21.95

The Guilfoyle Report
AG Editions
142 Bank Street
New York, NY 10014
(212) 929-0959
Quarterly; annual subscription $58;
    sample issue $7.
An outstanding newsletter for professional nature photographers, The Guilfoyle Report has excellent how-to and equipment articles, in-depth looks at photo markets and much valuable, timely information that makes it of great interest to any serious bird photographer.

The Natural Image
Lepp and Associates
Box 6240
Los Osos, CA 93412
(805) 528-7385
Quarterly; $16/year
This newsletter covers many topics of general interest to nature photographers, contains many informative articles on specific subjects and also has useful reviews of new products.

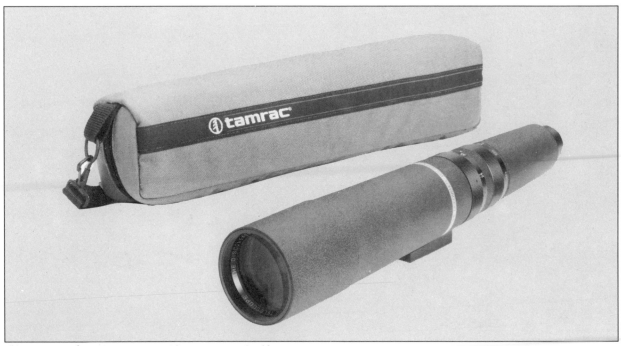

This scope case from Tamrac comes with a convenient shoulder strap.

The ultimate portable blind—the hat blind from Lepp and Associates. The blind folds up and fits into the helmet-style hat when not in use.

A blind is very useful for close observation. This camouflaged model is from Lepp and Associates.

2
BACKYARD BIRDING

Types of Feeders • Squirrel-Proofing • What to Feed the Birds • Feeding Hummingbirds • Landscaping for the Birds • Bird Baths • Bird Houses • Mail-Order Sources of Bird Supplies

TYPES OF FEEDERS

One of the many joys of feeding the birds is watching the antics of regular visitors. Hundreds of different feeders are on the market. They range from the general, designed for many kinds of birds and feed, to the highly specific, designed specifically for a single type of bird. Unfortunately, many bird feeders are more ornamental than functional. While ornamental is nice, functional will attract more birds—and a good combination of the two is ideal.

The choice of a feeder depends on many factors: location, type of feed, type of bird desired, capacity, and so on. In general, look for solid construction, whether in wood, metal or plastic. Contrary to popular belief, birds' feet and eyes will not freeze to metal feeders in the winter! The feeder should be easy to clean and fill, and should keep the seeds dry. For hanging feeders, be sure the ring or hook is solidly attached.

Wood feeders are often considered the most traditional and attractive. They have several advantages: they hold a lot of seed, many different kinds of birds can feed, and they are easy to fill. On the other hand, squirrels can easily chew them up, and the hanging kind are hard to squirrel-proof. In addition, large or undesirable birds can easily dominate the feeder, keeping smaller birds off. Birds on the far side of the feeder will be hard or impossible to see (also true of metal feeders).

Plastic feeders allow all the birds that land on them to be seen. They are easy to fill, clean and squirrel-proof, but they tend to have small capacities. Moisture from condensation can be trapped inside, leading to moldy seeds. When buying a plastic feeder, look for noncorrosive metal (preferably zinc) perches, trays, seed ports, base and cap. A good tough plastic such as Lexan is preferable for long life.

Hanging plastic tube feeders to hold

The Big Top model hanging feeder from Droll Yankees has no perches, so only small birds can feed. The baffle over the top shelters the seeds and keeps the squirrels away.

When squirrels or heavy birds such as crows try to get into this feeder from Looker Products, their own weight closes the seed tray.

Birds adore this extra-large thistle feeder from Presto Galaxy.

The squirrel baffle on this feeder from Droll Yankees can be lowered over the seeds to prevent unwanted large birds, such as grackles, from feeding.

sunflower seeds or thistle seeds are among the most popular. Perches are a must; a bottom tray to keep hulls and dropped seeds off the lawn is usually optional. If possible, purchase a tube feeder that has a separate seed hopper for each perch—this prevents fighting when the seed gets low. Thistle tubes are specifically designed for dispensing Niger (thistle) seed for finches, particularly goldfinches. They have very small holes that allow the finches to pull the seeds through but keep birds with large beaks from getting any. Niger seed will get moldy if not eaten quickly, so it may be preferable to purchase a thistle tube with a relatively small capacity.

Window feeders are a very enjoyable way to meet the birds. These feeders bring nature's creatures practically within touching distance, and allow easy observation without binoculars—a great way to introduce children to the joys of birdwatching. Window feeders are also enjoyed by many elderly and handicapped birdwatchers. Sometimes movement behind the window will frighten the birds off temporarily, but they will quickly return, and regular visitors may learn to ignore viewers. (Some birds—chickadees, most notoriously—are absolutely fearless at the feeder.) Most window feeders attach very simply with suction cups, which need to be replaced every six months or so. Some window feeders actually fit into the window and project into the house. A one-way coating on the projection allows close-up viewing without frightening the birds.

Small bird feeders are designed to keep birds like chickadees, titmice and nuthatches from being crowded out at tube or wooden feeders. To make it difficult for larger birds to land, these feeders have no perches. Some small bird feeders have an adjustable dome or some other system that lowers over the seed container to keep the large birds out; others have portholes to which the birds cling while feeding.

Suet feeders to attract woodpeckers and other birds should be made with vinyl-coated wire to prevent corrosion and rough edges. Other alternatives to hold the suet are mesh bags, logs or branches with holes drilled into them, and coconut shell halves. Any suet feeder that is not firmly attached has a good chance of disappearing in the middle of the night, carried off by a hungry raccoon. Sometimes other birds, particularly starlings, will dominate a suet feeder and keep the woodpeckers away. If this a problem, find a feeder that opens only on the bottom.

Other feeders of various sorts are commercially available. Feeders that hold apple or orange halves on spears are a good way to attract orioles, mockingbirds and catbirds in the summer. Peanut feeders will attract blue jays and titmice.

The Right Feeder

Because different birds have different feeding patterns, no one type of feeder will attract every sort of bird. For the most attractive feeding station, four different types will be needed.

Ground feeders. To attract ground-feeding birds such as sparrows, blue jays, juncos, towhees, mourning doves and pheasants, simply scatter the food on the ground. For the sake of aesthetics and tidiness, the food can be placed in a flat dish, on a board or in a slight depression in the grass. When snow is on the ground, scatter the food on top of it, preferably in a sheltered area (under the eaves, for example).

Post feeders. Many birds, including cardinals, chickadees, wrens, sparrows and grosbeaks, prefer to feed a few feet above ground level. Any of the myriad of post feeders available is a good choice to attract these birds. Food placed in a dish on a tree stump, table or windowsill will also be attractive.

Tree feeders. An excellent way to attract woodpeckers is to attach a suet feeder or peanut butter feeder to a tree at a height of about 5 to 6 feet (1.5 m to 2 m). This will also attract chickadees, titmice and brown creepers, among other birds.

Hanging feeders. Probably the most popular feeders are hanging feeders that attach to tree limbs or hang from poles or arms. Many, many different kinds are available. Most wooden hanging feeders can also be mounted on poles. Hanging feeders will attract birds that cling to the feeder while eating—chickadees, nuthatches, finches and titmice. The

Nuthatches are also fond of suet. The simple suet holder is from Duncraft.

year-round antics of these lively birds may be what make a feeder that actually attracts relatively few birds so popular.

Feeder Cautions

When many birds crowd together at bird feeders, the risk of spreading disease among them increases. If grain seeds are allowed to accumulate in or near the feeder, and they then get wet, a mold that causes the serious avian disease aspergillus can develop. Bird droppings can also spread diseases and parasites among birds at a feeder. To prevent disease, keep the feeder clean and the seed dry. Clean up spilled seed and discarded seed hulls from around the feeder.

A problem encountered by many backyard birders is birds crashing into windows. This is almost always caused by reflections. Sometimes the bird sees the reflection of the yard in the window and thinks it is flying into an open space; territorial birds may see their own reflections and try to chase off an "intruder." To solve the problem, move the feeder or break up the reflections by hanging something in the window. Wind chimes and mobiles are good choices.

Should a bird strike a window and be stunned, there is a good chance it will recover. If no other animals are around, just leave the bird alone; it will stay still or move around a little, and then fly away, usually within fifteen minutes or so. If cats or other possible predators are nearby, bring the bird indoors and invert a cardboard box over it. When the bird starts to move around in the box, it can be released.

Homemade Feeders

Bird feeders can be inexpensively improvised from almost anything. For post feeders, any shallow bowl or basket left out on a table or bench works well. A favorite way to feed suet or peanut butter is to put it onto a pine cone and then hang the cone from a branch. Imagination and what the birds accept are the only limitations.

Birds will join you at breakfast if you put up a window feeder. This model is from Duncraft.

This chalet-style window feeder is made by Aspects.

SQUIRREL-PROOFING

The most important thing to know about squirrel-proofing a bird feeder is that it can't be done. All sorts of ingenious and fairly effective baffles are available, but it takes more than a baffle to foil a determined squirrel—and all squirrels are *very* determined. To combat squirrels (and also chipmunks, raccoons and other pests) the feeder must be protected in all directions.

Because squirrels can jump astonishing distances straight up and to the sides, hanging or pole-mounted feeders must be placed at least 5 feet (1.5 m) above the ground and at least 10 feet (3 m) from any possible launching points to the sides—trees, decks, window sills, eaves and so on.

An effective way to keep squirrels from climbing up a pole is a sliding cylindrical pole baffle called a Squirrel Spooker Pole. This ingenious and inexpensive device has a sleeve that fits around the pole. When the squirrel grasps the sleeve below the feeder, it slides down the pole, usually causing the squirrel to jump off unharmed. A counterweight inside the pole returns the sleeve to its original position. A simpler method with fewer moving parts is a disk or dome baffle that fits on the pole below the feeder. A similar concept for hanging feeders involves a tilting dome that attaches above the feeder and keeps squirrels from climbing down onto it. It may be necessary to remove the bottom tray from hanging feeders, since this can give a squirrel something to grab.

Some feeder designs are very effective against squirrels: the Mandarin, Hylarious and Big Top are three excellent choices carried by many stores and mail-order sources.

If you can't beat the squirrels, try joining them. Ears of dried corn attached to a chain and hung from a branch will keep the squirrels away from the bird

If you can't beat them, join them. The Squirrel-a-Whirl from Wildlife Products provides hours of hilarity as the squirrels scramble for the corn.

feeder and incidentally provide a great deal of amusement to onlookers. Several hanging devices are available.

Individual squirrels or raccoons that are special pests can be humanely trapped and released in another location.

County extension agents can often provide information and instructions and will even lend traps. Remember, however, that removing a pesky squirrel may only open the way for another squirrel to take over the role.

WHAT TO FEED THE BIRDS

The goal of a feeder is to attract the biggest variety of birds and provide them with the maximum nutrition. What to put into the bird feeder is sometimes a confusing problem, particularly because commercial bird-food mixes can contain differing varieties of seeds. The most important types of seeds and seed mixes are discussed below.

Sunflower seeds. Large birds, small birds and birds in between all love sunflower seeds. There are two types: white-striped and black oil. The black oil seed has several advantages over the white-striped. It has a higher meat-to-shell ratio, it is more nutritious with a higher fat content and it is cheaper. Sunflower meats are more expensive than sunflower seeds in the shell, but there is no mess to clean up under the feeder. Sunflower seeds are particularly attractive to chickadees, cardinals, nuthatches, pine siskins, redpolls, titmice, finches, crossbills, and grosbeaks.

Safflower seeds. Birds that like sunflower seeds will also enjoy safflower seeds. Crows, grackles and squirrels don't like the taste, however, so safflower is a good choice if these are a problem. The drawback is that safflower seeds are considerably more expensive.

Thistle (Niger) seed. To attract goldfinches, house finches, purple finches, redpolls, pine siskins, juncos and indigo buntings, these tiny seeds are magic. Niger is more expensive than sunflower seed, and the price has been going up. Some manufacturers are now offering a cheaper "finch mix" that is about half Niger and half other small seeds. Birds will eat this and will also eat canary seed, but pure Niger is much preferable.

Millet. White proso millet is a good food for attracting ground-feeding birds such as doves, juncos and sparrows. Cardinals, painted buntings, pine siskins, purple finches, towhees, cowbirds and redpolls will also eat millet. Red millet is far less attractive to many birds. Yellow millet will attract finches.

Peanuts. Catbirds, mockingbirds, blue jays, chickadees, towhees, common flickers, grosbeaks, woodpeckers, titmice and nuthatches all like peanut hearts, particularly in cold weather. Many larger species of birds can crack open peanuts in the shell.

Peanut butter. Peanut butter spread on pine cones attracts chickadees, brown creepers and nuthatches, among other birds. Some people mix the peanut butter with corn meal, thinking that this will keep the birds from choking. Although this is just as delicious to the birds, it is not really necessary. There is little evidence to prove that birds can choke to death on peanut butter.

Cracked corn. Finely cracked yellow corn is enjoyed by many birds in the winter. It is very inexpensive. Whole corn attracts ducks and geese.

Other seeds. Nuthatches, cardinals, blue jays and other birds all enjoy seeds from melons and squash. Instead of discarding these in the kitchen, try putting them in the feeder tray instead.

Seed mixtures. Many inexpensive

A chickadee visits a hanging Cape feeder from Duncraft. Note the suet holder on the side.

A woodpecker enjoys suet laced with insects, available from Cockerum Oregon Insects.

commercial seed mixes sold in supermarkets and similar stores contain wheat, red millet and milo mixed with sunflower seeds. In the long run, these end up being more expensive, since the birds just flick aside everything but the sunflower seeds. Commercial mixes from reliable sources (see pages 60–61) are much better. Some are seasonal mixes, some are general mixes designed to attract a variety of birds, while others are meant to attract finches, cardinals, small birds and the like.

A good formula for a homemade general mix is 45 percent white proso millet, 35 percent black oil sunflower seeds and 20 percent safflower seeds. A slightly less expensive formula is 55 percent white proso millet, 35 percent finely cracked yellow corn and 10 percent black oil sunflower seeds.

Grit. Birds have no teeth to crush their food. Instead, all birds swallow bits of sand or gravel, which grinds the food in their gizzards. Although grit is crucial to a bird's health, it is often neglected by those who feed the birds. A small amount of commercial grit (usually finely crushed oyster shells) in a ratio of twenty parts seed to one part grit, or placed separately in a small dish by the feeder, will provide birds with this important addition to their diet.

Suet. Woodpeckers and other insect-eating birds such as chickadees and nuthatches will be attracted to suet, especially in the winter. Raw beef suet can be purchased at any good butcher. Ren-

dered suet, often sold in cakes or balls mixed with seeds or peanuts, can be purchased from any bird supply company. Rendered suet is better for summer feeding, since it will not become rancid as quickly. Even so, keep the suet feeder in the shade in the summer. To render suet at home, first chop it coarsely in a food processor. Melt the suet in a double boiler over low heat; remove it from the heat and let it cool until it is slightly hardened. Reheat until it is in liquid form again, and then pour it into muffin tins, empty tuna cans or the like to make suet cakes. Seeds, peanuts or other additions, such as raisins or fruit bits, can be placed into the container before pouring in the suet. Store extra cakes in the freezer.

Woodpeckers are attracted to suet in feeders like this hanging double one from Duncraft.

Hummingbirds are attracted by the color red, but there is no need to color the nectar. This window feeder is from Aspects.

Birds such as evening grosbeaks will come right to the window. Shown here are three window feeders from Aspects.

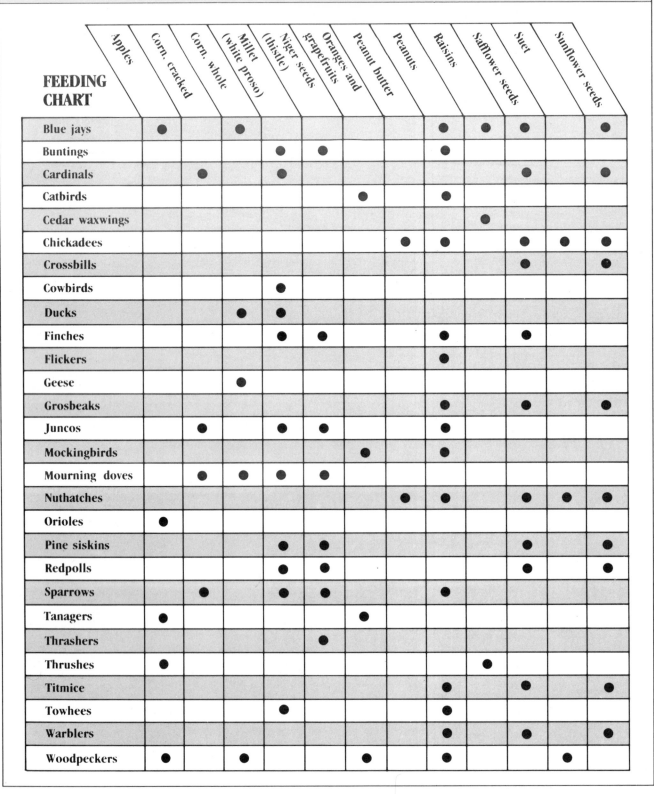

FEEDING CHART	Apples	Corn, cracked	Corn, whole	Millet (white proso)	Niger seeds (thistle)	Oranges and grapefruits	Peanut butter	Peanuts	Raisins	Safflower seeds	Suet	Sunflower seeds
Blue jays	●		●						●	●	●	●
Buntings				●	●				●			
Cardinals		●		●							●	●
Catbirds						●			●			
Cedar waxwings										●		
Chickadees								●	●		●	●
Crossbills											●	●
Cowbirds				●								
Ducks			●	●								
Finches				●	●				●		●	
Flickers									●			
Geese			●									
Grosbeaks									●		●	●
Juncos		●		●	●				●			
Mockingbirds							●		●			
Mourning doves		●	●	●	●							
Nuthatches								●	●		●	●
Orioles	●											
Pine siskins				●	●						●	●
Redpolls				●	●						●	●
Sparrows		●		●	●				●			
Tanagers	●						●					
Thrashers						●						
Thrushes	●									●		
Titmice									●		●	●
Towhees				●					●			
Warblers									●		●	●
Woodpeckers	●		●				●		●		●	

FEEDING HUMMINGBIRDS

Hummingbirds are found only in the Americas. These tiny birds dumbfounded the first European explorers, who thought at first they were a sort of insect. The average ruby-throated hummingbird is only 3½ inches long (9 cm) and weighs only one-sixth of an ounce (4.5 grams). By contrast, a house sparrow is about 5¼ inches (13 cm) long and weighs almost an ounce (27 grams). Of the 319 hummingbird species, only 15 are found in the United States. East of the Rockies only the ruby-throated hummingbird is likely to be seen. West of the Rockies, however, hummers are more common, and several different species can sometimes be seen at the same feeder. Hummingbirds are unpredictable—a feeder in one area may attract many while another feeder only a mile or so away will attract none. A garden full of hummers one year may have none the next.

To attract hummingbirds, hanging nectar feeders are preferred. They should be placed outdoors about May 1 or after frost is unlikely; they can be kept out into October. To get the birds accustomed to the feeder, hang it near flowering plants. Once the birds have learned about the feeder, it can be moved to a shady location with a better view. Dozens of hummingbird feeders are available. A good nectar feeder has several openings, since hummingbirds are highly territorial and will fight over the feeder. Look for feeders that are easy to open for refilling and cleaning. Bees and yellowjackets are also attracted to the nectar, so select a dripless feeder or one that has bee guards. To keep ants off the feeder, coat the hanging wire with petroleum jelly. There are many commercial nectars available. These are simple to mix with plain water and often contain a harmless red dye that is believed to help attract the birds, although this is debatable. To mix your own nectar, combine one part white sugar with four parts water and stir well until all the sugar is dissolved. Do not use honey—although it is not proven, many experts feel it can be harmful. Never use artificial sweeteners, which have no nutritional value. Fungus and bacteria will breed in the feeder if the nectar is not changed and the feeder not cleaned thoroughly each week.

Oriole feeders. If orioles are in the neighborhood, they can be attracted by offering jelly and sugar water. Specialized hanging feeders for orioles are available from many suppliers.

The Hummy-Bird Bar from Hummingbird Heaven is remarkably sturdy and quite inexpensive.

A downy woodpecker feasts on raw suet; the holder is from Duncraft.

The Winner window feeder from Droll Yankees attaches permanently with a bracket or temporarily with suction cups.

Feeders designed to attach to fences or patio railings, such as this model from Duncraft, bring the birds close to you and are easy to fill.

Duncraft sells this stocking feeder for thistle seeds.

LANDSCAPING FOR THE BIRDS

The next step beyond providing food and water for the birds is to landscape for them. By managing the backyard habitat you will attract a greater number and variety of birds than by feeding alone—and you will have a beautiful, if unconventional, property.

A broad expanse of pristine lawn is a traditional landscaping ideal, but it will attract few birds because it provides little food or cover. An open lawn has none of the tangle of trees, shrubs and vines that is found in natural habitats. Of course, this does not mean that only a jungle will attract birds. In fact, landscaping for the birds can be simple, inexpensive and beautiful if some basic principles are followed.

Edges. Where different habitats join is where the most bird life will be found—for example, where woodlands meet meadow, or where hedges and flowerbeds converge. Planting hedges is one way to add edges. Another good way is to let that part of the lawn adjoining woodland or hedges grow up into meadow. The wild flowers and grasses provide food and shelter.

Layering. Different birds prefer different elevations for feeding and nesting. Maximize this effect by putting in plantings of varying height: trees, shrubs, and herbaceous plants. For example, shade-tolerant shrubs can be planted near large trees. This will work especially well if the habitat has large, isolated trees.

Evergreens. Evergreen trees and shrubs are very important to birds, particularly for shelter in the winter. Owls are extremely fond of roosting and nesting in conifers; purple finches love to nest in ornamental evergreens. Plant a mixture of several kinds of evergreens to help the layering effect.

Neatness. A perfectly manicured garden will attract few birds. Tree stumps, dead branches, leaf litter, harvested garden plants and the like provide food for insect-eating birds, perches for them to roost on, and places to nest. Fruit-eating birds will eat apples, cherries, crabapples and other fruit that falls off the tree. Be less energetic about raking leaves, removing branches and windfalls and pruning the shrubbery.

Brushpiles. The shelter provided by a brushpile will draw many birds. A feeder that is out in the open and isn't visited much will show sharply increased activity if a brushpile is built nearby. Natural brushpiles are formed by the branches of fallen trees; a good artificial pile is easily made. Place a foundation of several logs or rows of rocks on the ground; mound large branches over the foundation, pointing the stems toward the ground. Smaller branches should be piled on top.

Plantings. Choose native trees and plants that are valuable to the birds: those that bear fruit, seeds, nuts or other foods (see the chart on page 54).

Contouring. Another way to attract birds is to vary the ground level, by building rock gardens, for example. Ground-feeding birds such as towhees will be attracted by the increased food possibilities.

Where To Find Help

Every state has a wildlife division staffed by specialists. The headquarters will be located in the state capital, and there may be regional or county offices. Write or call the nongame biologist; he or she will probably be able to provide detailed information about the appropriate bird-attracting plants for your state or region. In addition, the department can often provide bird checklists, brochures, bird house designs and other valuable information, usually for free or for a minimal charge.

The United States Department of Agriculture provides an excellent, inexpensive source of expert advice: the Cooperative Extension Service. Agents staff 3,165 offices, at least one in almost every county in the country; check the white pages of the telephone book under Cooperative Extension to find the office nearest you.

The Soil and Water Conservation Society publishes a catalog, *Sources of Native Seeds and Plants*. It is available for $3 from:

Soil and Water Conservation Society
7515 Northeast Ankeny Road
Ankeny, IA 50021

Flowers for Songbirds

amaranthus	foxtail
aster	millet
bachelor's button	hare's tail grass
black-eyed Susan	love-lies-bleeding
bluebell	marigold
calendula	moss rose
California poppy	phlox quaking
chrysanthemum	grass
coneflower	sunflower
coreopsis	verbena
cornflower	zinnia
cosmos	

Flowers for Hummingbirds

Hummingbirds are particularly attracted to red and orange flowers. When selecting varieties of the flowers listed below, choose those with the most vivid reds whenever possible.

beebalm	lupine
bugleweed	milkweed
columbine	morning glory
dahlia	nasturtium
fuschia	petunia
gladiolus	phlox
hibiscus	salvia
honeysuckle	snapdragon
impatiens	trumpet vine
larkspur	zinnia

Wildflower seed mixtures that are simply sprinkled over the soil are an easy and effective way to create bird-attracting meadows. This beautiful meadow was grown using the Songbird Meadow mix from White Swan.

White Swan's Songbird Meadow wildflower seed mix contains sunflowers, zinnias, asters, caiendulas, coreopsis, chrysanthemums, several other flowers and four ornamental grasses. White Swan also offers a specialized mixture called Hummingbird Garden.

Plantings for Birds Natural plantings that offer food and shelter are the best way to attract birds to a garden and keep them there. The chart below lists some suggested plantings.

	Northeast	Southeast	Northwest	Midwest	Southwest
Herbaceous Plants	creeping juniper panic grass strawberry sunflower Virginia creeper wild grape	cotoneaster bunchberry greenbrier panic grass sunflower	bearberry filaree fiddlenecks lupine sunflower tarweed timothy turkey mullein wintergreen	bearberry cotoneaster juniper strawberry woodbine	canyon grape fiddlenecks filaree honeysuckle lupine sunflower turkey mullein Virginia creeper woodbine
Low Shrubs	blackberry blueberry honeysuckle huckleberry raspberry snowberry	bayberry blackberry blueberry honeysuckle huckleberry lespedeza spicebush	blackberry blueberry buckthorn huckleberry Oregon grape serviceberry snowberry	buckthorn buffalo currant chokecherry hackberry	agarita blackberry buckthorn prickly pear spicebush thimbleberry Utah juniper
Tall Shrubs	autumn olive chokeberry dogwood elderberry sumac viburnum winterberry wisteria	dogwood elderberry juniper sumac	bitterbrush buckthorn Douglas hawthorn elderberry madrone Russian olive saltbush sumac	dogwood elder juniper sumac	hackberry lote bush madrone manzanita mountain ash mulberry saltbush sumac
Low Trees	apple cherry crabapple flowering dogwood hawthorn red cedar serviceberry	cherry dogwood hawthorn holly myrtle palmetto persimmon red cedar serviceberry	dogwood hawthorn mulberry paper birch serviceberry	Amur maple apple flowering crabapple mountain ash white mulberry	aspen chokecherry crabapple dogwood mesquite serviceberry

Tall Trees	**Coniferous:**
	balsam fir
	Colorado spruce
	hemlock
	huckleberry
	white pine
	Deciduous:
	beech
	birch
	holly
	red mulberry
	red oak
	sassafras
	sugar maple
	tulip
	white oak
		Coniferous:
		loblolly pine
		longleaf pine
		shortleaf pine
		slash pine
		Deciduous:
		ash
		beech
		black gum
		hackberry
		hickory
		live oak
		pecan
		southern red oak
		walnut
			Coniferous:
			Colorado white
			  spruce
			Douglas fir
			lodgepole pine
			ponderosa pine
			shore pine
			western white pine
			Deciduous:
			bigleaf maple
			California black
			  oak
			Oregon white oak
				Black gum
				  (sour gum)
				Black walnut
				Elm
				Hackberry
				Maple
				Pin Oak
				Sweet gum
				White oak
					Coniferous:
					Arizona cypress
					Colorado blue
					  spruce
					juniper
					piñon pine
					ponderosa pine
					Deciduous:
					bitter cherry
					cottonwood
					madrone
					live oak
					pine oak
					sycamore
					willow

BIRD BATHS

Birds need water all year round, not just in the summer. In fact, they may need it more in the winter, when all the water is frozen into ice. A bird bath is an excellent way to provide the birds with a need that is just as important as food. Many kinds of bird baths are available in a great range of prices. Baths should be shallow. If the bath has a flat floor, it should be no more than 1 inch deep. If the bath has a sloping floor, the grade must be very gentle, dropping to no deeper than 3 inches at the deepest point. Sloping basins should have ridges or grooves to keep the birds from slipping. The traditional bird bath is a pedestal-mounted basin with a diameter of about 16 inches (41 cm). In part this style is popular because the birds are in less danger from predators when they use it. Nonetheless, birds actually seem to prefer bird baths at ground level. Ground-level bird baths can be easily improvised from almost anything that will hold water (an old pie plate, for instance), as long as it meets the shallowness requirement. A number of very beautiful ornamental ground-level bird baths, made from stone, terra cotta and similar materials, are available. They can be placed in a flowerbed, on the edge of a terrace, or anywhere else.

Bird Bath Accessories

Keeping the water in the bird bath from freezing in winter is important. Some bird baths come with a built-in heater. Those that don't can easily be kept ice-free with specially designed electric heating element. Never put antifreeze in the bird bath!

The sound of running water is very attractive to birds. If a bubbler or drip spout of some sort is added to provide that sound, there will be as many birds at the bath as at the feeder. Several devices of this sort, designed to run off the garden faucet, are available.

The sound of running or dripping water magically attracts birds. This post-mounted birdbath with dripper is from Duncraft.

Duncraft carries this birdbath with mister—a good way to attract birds and to observe some interesting behavior.

BIRD HOUSES

The only birds that will be attracted to bird houses are those that normally build their nests in cavities such as hollow trees, old woodpecker holes and so on. The birds most easily attracted to bird houses are chickadees, bluebirds, wrens, purple martins, and tree swallows. Occasionally titmice, nuthatches, house finches, woodpeckers and owls will nest in bird houses. It is far more likely, however, that a house will be taken over by house sparrows or starlings. The best way to attract desirable birds is to provide the right sort of house. Listed below are some specific requirements for particular species.

With the exception of purple martin houses, bird houses should be made of wood. No other material is as good for providing the right temperature and ventilation. Birds are most attracted to houses that are tan, brown or gray. Houses should never be painted with creosote or lead-based paints. Creosote in particular is very toxic to birds. The interior of the house should never be painted at all. Drainage and ventilation are important in bird houses. Look for drainage holes in the bottom of the house and vent holes in the sides under the roof. To avoid wetness, the roof should extend a minimum of 3 inches (8 cm) beyond the entrance hole.

If old nests are left in a bird house over the winter, they will attract mice, who will then take over the house. Clean the house at the end of the season. Remove the old nests and wash the box if possible to help control parasites. This is easiest to do with houses that open from the sides.

Chickadees and Wrens

To keep sparrows out of houses meant for chickadees and wrens, the house should have an opening of 1⅛ inch (3 cm) in diameter and interior dimensions of approximately 6 × 6 × 8 ½ inches (15 × 15 × 22 cm). It should also have no perch, since perches make in-

This small redwood cottage from Duncraft is ideal for bluebirds or chickadees.

The Duncraft redwood lodge for small birds can be mounted on a tree or post.

A chickadee settles in at this birdhouse from Duncraft.

An eastern bluebird from Maslowski Wildlife Productions.

vasion by sparrows easier. The house should be placed 6 to 10 feet (2 to 3 m) above the ground to keep away marauding cats and raccoons. Chickadees will be especially attracted if the box is filled with wood shavings.

Bluebirds

At one time bluebirds were a common garden bird, nesting in dead trees and old wooden fence posts. As these be-

came increasingly scarce, so did the bluebirds. To help reverse this trend, more and more backyard bird-lovers are putting up bluebird houses. A desirable house has an opening 1½ inches (4 cm) in diameter, ample interior space (5 × 5 × 8 inches [13 × 13 × 20 cm] or larger) and is well ventilated. Because sparrows and starlings will find the house equally desirable, it should be constructed in way that makes it easy

to open to evict unwelcome squatters— something that will have to be done often. For the best chance of attracting bluebirds, mount several boxes about 100 yards (90 m) apart on fence posts or the like 4 to 6 feet (1 to 2 m) high. The ideal environment is along the edges of open fields such as pastures, golf courses and cemeteries.

Purple Martins

The largest North American swallows, purple martins live communally. Because their diet consists of flying insects that are caught on the wing, a purple martin colony is a good way to help keep down the backyard population of mosquitos and other flying insect pests. It is claimed that a single purple martin can eat 2,000 mosquitos in one day.

Today virtually all purple martin colonies in America nest in housing provided by humans. To attract these graceful birds the right habitat is important. A large, open yard with water such as a pond or stream is ideal. A less than optimal yard that is located near a colony in a good yard will also attract purple martins. However, even a good habitat may not immediately attract a colony. Some purple martin landlords have good luck right away, while others must wait patiently for several seasons before the martins discover the property.

Good martin houses are usually made of aluminum or wood, although throughout the South and Southwest purple martins happily nest in hollow gourds hung from trees. Aluminum is preferred because it is lighter. There are many charming martin house designs available, in sizes ranging from six to twenty-four nesting compartments, with twelve being the most popular. Many designs feature add-on floors to accommodate the colony as it grows. Most also feature railed balconies that allow baby birds to walk around safely; adults perch on the rails. As with any other bird house, takeover attempts by sparrows a constant problem. Eternal vigilance is the price of a martin colony; the sparrow nests must be removed every few days in the spring. However, since a purple martin house should be mounted on a pole about 15 feet (4.5 m) above the ground, this can be a problem. The house must be mounted in a way that allows it to be easily lowered and raised. Several systems are available; most use telescoping poles or poles with pulleys. The choice is really one of individual

The Trio Grandpa martin house can be raised and lowered using a lanyard system. It has twelve apartments.

convenience. Almost all aluminum purple martin houses have flip-up doors on the compartments to make clearing out the sparrows easier. A roof perch, which allows the martins to congregate on the house, is an important feature to have.

Purple martins winter in Brazil. The first scouts generally arrive in mid- to late March to seek out housing, so it pays to have the house ready in advance. The scouts fly back and return with the rest of the colony in mid- to late April; nesting begins at once. By mid-July the fledglings are out of the nest, and in mid-August the colony begins the long journey back to Brazil.

Nuthatches and Downy Woodpeckers

Both nuthatches and downy woodpeckers will nest in houses with interior dimensions of roughly 6 × 6 × 12 inches (15 × 15 × 30 cm). Attach the house to tree at a height of between 6 and 20 feet. Downies and nuthatches

are year-round residents, so they will also roost in the house in the winter.

Redheaded and Hairy Woodpeckers

Houses for redheaded and hairy woodpeckers should have an entrance hole with a diameter of 2 inches (5 cm) and interior dimensions of about 8 × 8 × 15 inches (20 × 20 × 38 cm). Mount the houses about 10 to 15 feet (3 to 4.5 m) high in a wooded area.

Roosting Boxes

Where do the birds go on a stormy winter's night? To roost boxes, if they can. Designed simply for shelter, roost boxes can be mounted, preferably in a sheltered area, at fence-post height or in trees. The interior should have staggered perches so that the birds don't have to roost on top of each other. The entrance hole should have a perch and a diameter of about 1½ inches (4 cm); it should be placed near the bottom of the box to help keep in the birds' body heat.

The Trio Castle is the biggest purple martin house available—it has twenty-four compartments.

Bird Emergencies

Occasionally an injured, abandoned or captured bird crosses the path of a bird lover. Here's what to do:

Injured birds. An injured or sick bird is best left on its own, to recover or not as part of the natural order. However, if you must help the bird, the best thing is to contact the people who know what to do—the local ASPCA, Humane Society, Audubon Society or state wildlife official. Caring for an injured bird is a specialized task; leave it to those who have the necessary experience.

Under federal law *all* birds (except starlings and house sparrows) are protected. It is illegal to keep protected animals of any sort in captivity unless a special license is obtained.

Abandoned birds. A baby bird apparently on its own is often thought to be orphaned. This is unlikely—a parent bird is almost certainly nearby and there is no need for concern. It is best simply to leave the bird alone. If a young bird has obviously fallen out of a nest, however, place it back. The belief that the parent bird will reject the baby because it has been touched by humans is completely unfounded—birds have a very poor sense of smell. If the entire nest has fallen down, try to replace it.

Captured birds. Otherwise well-behaved cats and dogs will sometimes catch a bird. If the bird is still alive, chances are it is not seriously harmed. Simply release the bird; return a fledgling to the area of the nest, if possible.

MAIL-ORDER SOURCES OF BIRD SUPPLIES

There are surprisingly few retail stores that specialize in supplies for backyard birdwatchers. Sacks of bird seed can often be purchased in pet-food stores; feed, feeders, baths and so on are often sold in garden centers. However, the selection is often limited. National Audubon Society chapters and other local bird clubs sometimes sell seeds. The best way to find good seeds and a wide choice of equipment is through a specialized mail-order supplier. The prices, selection, quality and service of the sources listed below are generally good.

All Supplies (including food)

Audubon Workshop
1501 Paddock Drive
Northbrook, IL 60062
(312) 729-6660

BackYard Birds & Co.
717 South Broadway
Springfield, MO 65804
(417) 869-4788

Duncraft
Penacook, NH 03303
(603) 224-0200

Princess Anne Farmers Service
5651 Virginia Beach Boulevard
Norfolk, VA 23502
(804) 461-1580

The Wild Bird Shop
1511 West 350 North
West Lafayette, IN 47906
(317) 463-2098

Wild Bird Supplies
4815 Oak Street
Crystal Lake, IL 60012
(815) 455-4020

Wild Birds Unlimited
1430 Broad Ripple Avenue
Indianapolis, IN 46220
(317) 251-5904
This company also has over fifteen franchised retail shops in Michigan, Wisconsin, Ohio and Indiana.

Feeders and Houses

Aspects
Box 408
Warren, RI 02885
(401) 247-1854

The Aviarium
Box 158
South Yarmouth, MA 02664
(617) 394-9194

Droll Yankees
Mill Road
Foster, RI 02825
(401) 647-3324

Heath Manufacturing Company
Box 105
Coopersville, MI 49404
(800) 678-8183/(616) 837-8181

Hummingbird Heaven
1255 Carmel Drive
Simi Valley, CA 93065
Hummingbird and oriole feeders only.

Rudolf Kopecky
1220 Ridge Road
Hypoluxo, FL 33462

Looker Products
Box 29
Milford, IL 60953
(815) 889-4042

Mapes Industries
6 Grace Avenue, Suite 404
Great Neck, NY 11021
(516) 487-7995

C&S Products
Box 848
Fort Dodge, IA 50501
(800) 255-2255
Suet and suet accessories only

Seaboard Seed Company
Bristol, IL 60512
(800) 323-1862/(312) 553-5800
Exclusive manufacturer and distributor of National Audubon Society Premium wild bird food.

Stylistic Services
Box 6359
Fullerton, CA 92634
(714) 525-8004
Hummingbird nectar.

Bird Bath Heaters

Nelson Manufacturing Company
3049 Twelfth Street SW
Cedar Rapids, IA 52406
(319) 363-2607
Manufacturers of Blue Devil heaters.

Nature House, Inc.
Purple Martin Junction
Griggsville, IL 62340
(217) 833-2323
Manufacturer of Trio system purple
  martin houses only.

North States Industries
3650 Fremont Avenue North
Minneapolis, MN 55412
(612) 522-6505

Presto Galaxy
255 Banker Street
Greenpoint, NY 11222
(800) 233-4447/(718) 389-7500

Wildlife Products
Box 363
Wisconsin Rapids, WI 54495
(715) 423-3737

Specialized Foods

Cockerum Oregon Insects
Box 714
Tillamook, OR 97141
(503) 842-5988
Beef-kidney suet blocks containing
  insects are very attractive to insect-
  eating birds such as nuthatches and
  woodpeckers. The company also offers
  Oregon Bluebird Meal, a mixture of
  ground grains, suet, insects and
  chopped dried apples that bluebirds
  find delicious.

The vinyl-coated wire lattice on this tube feeder from Duncraft fences out the squirrels but lets small birds like this tufted titmouse feed easily.

3
INFORMATION AND SOURCES

The National Audubon Society • The Cornell Laboratory of Ornithology • Organizations for Birdlovers • Great Birders in American History • Field Guides and Other Reading • Bookstores for Birders • Periodicals • Bird Recordings and Videos • Bird Slides • Birding Hotlines

THE NATIONAL AUDUBON SOCIETY

A conservation organization with more than 550,000 members, the National Audubon Society works toward the preservation and wise use of America's natural heritage. The society's roots go back to 1886, when George Bird Grinnell, editor of the magazine *Forest And Stream*, formed the first American bird association, the Audubon Society, to protest the wholesale slaughter of birds by market gunners and for their plumes. The public was so responsive that Grinnell was overwhelmed and had to disband the association almost as soon as it was started. Others took up the challenge, however, and formed state societies. The Massachusetts and Pennsylvania Audubon Societies were formed in 1896; by 1899, fifteen others had formed.

These separate groups formed the National Committee of Audubon Societies, an informal alliance, in 1901. In 1905, they formally created the National Association of Audubon Societies for the Protection of Wild Birds and Animals. The name was changed to National Audubon Society in 1940.

From the beginning, the society has been involved with education and conservation. In 1900 the society began hiring wardens to patrol and protect nesting and breeding sites, such as Mantinicus Rock in Maine. Three wardens were killed in the line of duty. The first national wildlife refuge was created in 1903 on Pelican Island in Florida at the urging of the society. The Audubon refuge system began around then, too. The largest Audubon refuge, the 26,000-acre Paul J. Rainey Sanctuary in Louisiana, was acquired in 1924.

By the 1930s the society had begun to sponsor scientific research about such endangered birds as the roseate spoonbill and ivory-billed woodpecker. These programs were extended in later decades to include California condors, large

The use of birds—in this case, an arctic tern—and feathers for hat decorations was so widespread in the late 1800s and early 1900s that it threatened many species with extinction.

The ladies of the Los Angeles Audubon Society gather in 1918.

wading birds, bald eagles, peregrine falcons and others.

Pesticide control and environmental protection have been important issues to the Society since the 1960s. An office in Washington, D.C. was opened in 1969 to lobby for environmental legislation. Current concerns include the problems of acid rain, habitat destruction and species extinction.

Participants at a National Audubon Society summer camp in Maine.

Warden Guy Bradley was murdered in the line of duty in 1905 by plume hunters in Florida. His tragic death became a rallying point for conservationists.

Audubon Today

The National Audubon Society today has more than 500 chapters and also staffs ten regional offices. Its national sanctuary system protects more than 250,000 acres, and hundreds of additional acres are protected by local chapters. Six education centers, four summer ecology camps, the Audubon Expedition Institute and field seminars are all part of the ongoing education programs. Field research on endangered species is an important part of the society's work. Conferences, workshops, seminars and a publishing program for scientific journals and papers are all part of the scientific activities.

The Lillian Annette Rowe Bird Sanctuary along the Platte River in Nebraska is used by sandhill cranes, whooping cranes, bald eagles and large numbers of migratory waterfowl.

Publications

Frank Chapman, an ornithologist at the American Museum of Natural History, began publishing a magazine called *Bird-Lore* in 1899. After the National Association of Audubon Societies was formed, *Bird-Lore* was offered to the members and also to the teachers who organized the thousands of Junior Audubon clubs in schools across the nation (this program involved some four million children over its twenty-five-year existence!). In 1935 the society bought the magazine from the museum and changed the name to *Audubon Magazine* in 1940. The covers were painted by Roger Tory Peterson, then on the staff. Also in 1940 the society began the technical journal *Audubon Field Notes*,

now known as *American Birds*. Today *Audubon* offers wonderful articles about the natural world, magnificently illustrated with stunning, full-color photographs. *American Birds*, while more technical and dealing only with birds, is equally beautiful. Another important society publication is *Audubon Activist*, a lively, bimonthly tabloid covering critical environmental issues.

The Christmas Bird Count

The Christmas Bird Count began on Christmas Day in 1900, when Frank Chapman organized twenty-five groups in the Northeast as a protest against the traditional holiday slaughter in which teams competed to see who could shoot the most birds in one day. Today the

National Audubon Society sponsors its annual Christmas Bird Count every year from December 17 to January 3. This event enlists the aid of over 41,000 birdwatchers in every state, every province of Canada and several countries in South America, Central America and the Caribbean islands. Participants spend an entire day, regardless of weather, taking a census of the birds in their region.

Every bird that can be identified is listed and later reported to Audubon. Every year some 1,200 different species are identified, and well over 74 million individual birds are counted by over 1,500 groups.

The data provide critical information about the winter distribution of resident bird species and allow researchers to track changes in bird populations and ranges. The Christmas Bird Count is organized by *American Birds,* which devotes a book-sized issue every year to analyzing the results.

Any birder wishing to participate in a Christmas Bird Count should contact a local Audubon Society chapter or write to the Christmas Bird Count Editor at *American Birds.* Many counts are held on a Saturday or Sunday; a modest fee of a few dollars is collected to help defray expenses. Each count area is a unique circle 15 miles (24 km) in diameter, encompassing about 175 square miles (455 km^2). Groups try to cover as much territory within the circle as is possible within the twenty-four hours of a single calendar day. Not surprisingly, some groups devote weeks to planning the logistics in order to claim the longest list of birds. The record is 326, noted in the Atlantic Canal Area of Panama in 1986. Some counters have been known to travel by dogsled to find their birds. Those who are less adventurous and live within the count circle can participate in a more leisurely fashion by recording the birds that visit their bird feeders during the course of the count day.

Birdathons

During Audubon Month every April, the National Audubon Society sponsors Birdathons across the country. These competitive bird counts are held between April 1 and May 30, depending on the peak migration at the particular locales. Sponsors pledge money for each bird a participant spots during the chosen twenty-four-hour period; participants also compete for awards and donated prizes. The proceeds are used to help finance local Audubon conservation projects and also support the National Audubon Society's sanctuaries, research, education and lobbying efforts. Anyone can participate in a Birdathon by going on a field trip, watching a backyard feeder or being a sponsor. For information about dates and locations for Birdathons, contact the Audubon Birdathon Coordinator at the national headquarters.

National Audubon Society researcher Dr. Carl Safina bands a common tern.

Audubon on the Air

The Audubon Television Specials, a series of award-winning documentaries about the natural world, offer viewers a look at the wonders of nature while stressing the need for conservation. The series is co-produced by the National Audubon Society, Turner Broadcasting System and WETA/TV, the public television station in Washington, DC; it is supported by a major grant from the Stroh Brewery Company. There are four new programs every year. Each first airs four times on cable SuperStation TBS and then runs again on PBS stations nationwide over the summer. Recent programs include "Wood Stork: Barometer of the Everglades," "Condor," "Ducks Under Siege" and "Countdown to Zero." Videocassettes of the shows are available for use in classrooms and libraries. For more information, contact:

WETA/TV
Box 2626
Washington, DC   20013

Audubon Education

Audubon Adventures, the youth education program of the National Audubon Society, is a new school program that provides children in grades three through six with a greater understanding and appreciation of the natural world. Some 170,000 children participate in programs through nearly 6,000 clubs.

Audubon ecology and nature camps have been in operation for over fifty years. Programs are offered on a variety of topics at several locations, ranging from children's sessions in Maine to wilderness research in Wyoming. Some sessions offer college credit. For more information, contact:

Audubon Ecology Camps
and Workshops
613 Riversville Road
Greenwich, CT   06831

Alexander Sprunt, vice president for field research at the National Audubon Society, holds a white-crowned pigeon.

National Audubon Society Offices

National Office
950 Third Avenue
New York, NY   10022
(212) 832-3200

Capital Office
645 Pennsylvania Avenue, SE
Washington, DC   20003
(202) 547-9009

Alaska
308 G Street, Suite 217
Anchorage, AK   99501
(907) 276-7034

Central Midwest
(Illinois, Indiana, Kentucky, Michigan,
   Ohio, Tennessee)
444 Barker Road
Michigan City, IN   46360
(219) 879-3227

Mid-Atlantic
(Delaware, Washington, DC, Maryland,
   New Jersey, Pennsylvania, Virginia,
   West Virginia)
1104 Fernwood Avenue, Suite 300
Camp Hill, PA   17011
(717) 763-4985

North Midwest
(Iowa, Minnesota, North Dakota,
   Wisconsin)
Suite 330, City Place
730 Hennepin Avenue
Minneapolis, MN   55403
(612) 375-9140

Northeast
(Connecticut, Maine, Massachusetts, New
   Hampshire, New York, Rhode Island,
   Vermont)
Northeast Audubon Center
Route 1, Box 171
Sharon, CT   06069
(203) 364-0520

Rocky Mountain
(Arizona, Colorado, Idaho, Montana,
   Utah, Wyoming)
4150 Darley, Suite 5
Boulder, CO   80303
(719) 499-0219

Southeast
(Alabama, Florida, Georgia, Mississippi,
   North Carolina, Puerto Rico, South
   Carolina)
Box 1268
Charleston, SC   29402
(803) 723-6171

Southwest
(Louisiana, New Mexico, Texas, Mexico)
2525 Wallingwood, Suite 1505
Austin, TX   78746
(512) 327-1943

West Central
(Arkansas, Kansas, Missouri, Nebraska,.
*   Oklahoma)*
210 South Wind Place
Manhattan, KS   66502
(913) 537-4385

Western
(California, Guam, Hawaii, Nevada,
*   Oregon, Washington)*
555 Audubon Place
Sacramento, CA   95825
(916) 481-5332

Audubon Publications

All Audubon publications originate in the national office in New York City.

Audubon Magazine
Les Line, editor
Published six times a year. Included in
*   cost of membership; subscriptions*
* $16 annually; single issues $3.*

Audubon Action
Bimonthly newsletter of society
*   activities. Included in cost of*
*   membership.*

American Birds
Susan Roney Drennan, editor
Published five times a year. Subscription
* $27.50 annually; includes Christmas*
*   Bird Count issue.*

Audubon Activist
Published six times a year. Subscription
* $9 annually; includes membership in*
*   Audubon Activist Network.*

Other Publications

Helpful booklets such as "Banquets for Birds" and "A Beginner's Guide to Birdwatching" are available from the Conservation Information department.

The comfortable viewing area of the Lyman Stuart Bird Observatory at the Cornell Lab of Ornithology.

Two researchers from the Cornell Laboratory of Ornithology gather specimens on a Long Island beach.

Ducks at the Cornell Laboratory of Ornithology's Sapsucker Woods Bird Sanctuary.

Membership in the National Audubon Society

Membership in the National Audubon society includes membership in the nearest local chapter of over 500 Audubon chapters nationwide. Chapters offer natural history field trips, bird walks, films and talks, a newsletter, the company of people with similar interests and the opportunity to work on current issues. Membership also brings six yearly issues of both *Audubon Magazine* and *Audubon Action,* a monthly newsletter covering the society's activities. All members are admitted free to National Audubon Nature Centers. An individual membership is $30, family membership is $38, and student membership is $18. Individual senior citizens can become members for $21; senior citizen families can join for $23. For membership information, contact:

Membership Data Center
Box 2667
Boulder, CO   80321

A sandhill crane, one of the crane species protected by the International Crane Foundation.

The Audubon Cause

The goals of the National Audubon Society can be stated as follows:

- Conserve native plants and animals and their habitats.
- Promote rational strategies for energy development and use, stressing conservation and renewable energy sources.
- Protect life from pollution, radiation and toxic substances.
- Further the wise use of land and water.
- Seek solutions for global problems involving the interaction of populations, resources and the environment.

Perhaps the best examples of these goals in practical application are the society's high-priority campaigns. Ongoing projects include opposing development in the Arctic National Wildlife Refuge, amending the Clean Air Act, preserving old forests, preserving the Platte River and preserving wetlands.

Wildlife Sanctuaries

The National Audubon Society owns and operates too many sanctuaries to list here. Not all the sanctuaries are even open to the public. Some are closed to the public because the presence of people will disturb the wildlife—nesting birds, for example. Others are closed simply because they are inaccessible. A number of sanctuaries are open, but arrangements must be made in advance—at some locations, the warden must pick up visitors in a boat. The sanctuaries listed below are just some of those easily available to the public. For more information contact:

**National Audubon Society
Sanctuary Department**
RR 1, Box 294
West Cornwall Road
Sharon, CT   06069
(203) 364-0048

Dauphin Island Sanctuary
Box 189
Dauphin Island, AL   365228
(205) 861-2882

**Richardson Bay Wildlife Sanctuary
and Whittell Education Center**
376 Greenwood Beach Road
Tiburon, CA   94920
(415) 388-2524

**Audubon Center in Greenwich and
Fairchild Wildflower Garden**
613 Riversville Road
Greenwich, CT   06830
(203) 869-5272

Miles Wildlife Sanctuary
RR 1, Box 295
West Cornwall Road
Sharon, CT   06069
(203) 364-5302

Northeast Audubon Center
RR 1, Box 171
Sharon, CT   06069
(203) 364-0520

Corkscrew Swamp Sanctuary
Box 1875A, Route 6
Sanctuary Road
Naples, FL   33964
(813) 657-3771

Rookery Bay Sanctuary
3967 North Road
Naples, FL   33942
(813) 774-2922

Clyde E. Buckley Sanctuary
RR 3
Frankfort, KY   40601
(606) 873-5711

**Jefferson County Forest Audubon
Sanctuary**
c/o Herb Zimmerman
Box 22348
Louisville, KY   40222

P.W. Sprague Memorial Sanctuary
c/o Mrs. Charles Lee
Box 3163
Prout's Neck, ME   04074
(207) 883-2133

Northwoods Audubon Center
Route 1
Sandstone, MN   55072
(612) 245-2648

**Palmer Lewis Sanctuary
Ramsey Hunt Wildlife Sanctuary
Ruth Walgreen Franklin and
Winifred Fels Audubon
Sanctuaries**
c/o Allen Kurtz
RD 1, Box 396
Mahopac, NY   10541
(914) 628-8061

Theodore Roosevelt Sanctuary
134 Cove Road
Oyster Bay, NY   11771
(516) 922-3200

Aullwood Audubon Center and Farm
1000 Aullwood Road
Dayton, OH   45414
(513) 890-7360

Crosswicks
Wyncote Audubon Society
Box 2
Wyncote, PA   19095

Francis Beidler Forest
Route 1, Box 114
Harleyville, SC   29448
(803) 462-2150

Sabal Palm Grove
Box 8277
Brownsville, TX   78520
(512) 541-8034

Schlitz Audubon Center
111 East Brown Deer Road
Milwaukee, WI   53217
(414) 352-2880

THE CORNELL LABORATORY OF ORNITHOLOGY

The Laboratory of Ornithology at Cornell University in Ithaca, New York, was founded in 1955 by two eminent ornithologists, Professor Arthur A. Allen and Professor Peter Paul Kellogg. Dr. Allen was a pioneering bird photographer; Dr. Kellogg was a leader in birdsong recording. The innovative programs begun by these two men established the laboratory as an important center for bird study. Today the laboratory is a nonprofit membership organization dedicated to the study and appreciation of birds.

The Library of Natural Sounds and the Division of Visual Services continue to lead in their fields, and the laboratory has expanded tremendously. Current programs monitor bird populations, study bird biology and management, help save endangered species and foster communication and collaboration between birdwatchers and professional ornithologists. The laboratory has a 200-acre (80 ha) sanctuary at Sapsucker Woods, open to the public. Four miles (6 km) of trails wind through the varied terrain. The Lyman K. Stuart Observatory at Sapsucker Woods has a huge picture window overlooking a 10-acre pond. Outdoor microphones bring the sounds of nature inside. The observatory also has exhibits and displays; original art by many renowned artists hangs in the hallways. The Crow's Nest Bookshop carries a very broad selection of books, recordings and other bird-related materials, as well as gifts and art reproductions. The laboratory's famed magazine, *The Living Bird Quarterly,* comes with membership. For more information, contact the laboratory at:

159 Sapsucker Woods Road
Ithaca, NY   14850
(607) 254-BIRD

Research Programs

Thousands of enthusiastic birdwatchers participate in aspects of the Cooperative Research Program. Participants in the Nest Record Program and the Colonial Birds Register, for example, find bird nests and colonies in the field and record information about them on data cards. The information is compiled and analyzed at the laboratory to provide a comprehensive picture of the distribution, nesting habits and population trends of many species. The Cooperative Research Program also analyzes data from the Christmas Bird Counts, breeding bird censuses and winter bird population studies sponsored by the National Audubon Society.

The laboratory manages the world's largest ongoing study of bird migration. Birds from a loft of over 2,000 homing pigeons are released periodically throughout New York state, and how they find their way home is studied.

A wild turkey is released into the woods by National Wild Turkey Federation researchers.

The Seatuck Research Project on Long Island, New York, studies the effects of suburban development on animal and bird life and devises management techniques to preserve the birds in the suburban environment.

The Library of Natural Sounds

The largest collection of birdsong recordings in the world is found in the Library of Natural Sounds. The recordings are made in the field by members of the library staff and by a network of professional and amateur affiliates located throughout the world. The library supplies sounds for such projects as the *Peterson Field Guide to Bird Songs* and other recordings. In addition, the library has a large collection of the sounds of other animals, including whales, elephants and insects. The sounds are supplied to researchers, birdwatchers and business clients needing them for movie soundtracks and the like.

Complementing the work of the Library of Natural Sounds is the Bioacoustics Research Program, which studies animal sounds to understand how animals communicate.

Courses and Tours

Week-long courses in bird study, birdsong recording and nature photography are offered many summers. Home-study courses in bird biology and bird photography are also offered (see pages 235 and 236). Birding tours to various parts of the world, led by experts, are sponsored every year.

Project FeederWatch

In 1976, the Long Point Bird Observatory in Canada began a backyard feeder survey in Ontario. The survey provided useful information about bird populations, ranges and movements. In 1987, the survey's organizer, Erica Dunn, wanted to expand the survey to cover all of North America. Such a huge project required thousands of participants and sophisticated computers to analyze the data. The logical place to take the proposal was the Laboratory of Ornithology's program in Bird Population Studies. An agreement was soon reached, and in 1987 Project FeederWatch was launched. The project is a cooperative effort between the Laboratory of Ornithology and the Long Point Bird Observatory, and is sponsored by *Bird Watcher's Digest* magazine.

In its first year, Project FeederWatch drew over 4,000 participants. Every state in the United States has at least one participant, and all but three states have more than ten. Watchers observe the birds that visit their feeders on one or two days every two weeks throughout the winter. The numbers are recorded on special forms that are then sent on to the laboratory for analysis. Participants need not be expert birdwatchers, but they should be able to identify the birds that commonly visit their feeders. To enroll, send $9 along with your name and address to:

Project FeederWatch
Cornell Laboratory of Ornithology
159 Sapsucker Woods Road
Ithaca, NY   14850

In return, you will receive instructions, data forms, the newsletter *FeederWatch News,* the Project FeederWatch annual report and a great deal of satisfaction.

A peregrine falcon feasts on a gull at Padre Island, Texas. The Peregrine Fund has helped save these birds from extinction.

Workers from the National Wild Turkey Federation begin a reforestation project to restore the wild turkey's habitat.

Researchers from the Cornell Laboratory of Ornithology record bird songs in the field for the Library of Natural Sounds.

ORGANIZATIONS FOR BIRD LOVERS

American Birding Association
Box 6599
Colorado Springs, CO   80934
(719) 634-7736

American Federation of Aviculture
2208-A Artesia Boulevard
Box 1568
Redondo Beach, CA   90278
(213) 372-2988

The American Ornithologists' Union
c/o Division of Birds
National Museum of Natural History
Washington, DC   20560
(202) 357-1300

Association of Field Ornithologists
c/o Sarah B. Laughlin
Vermont Institute of Natural Science
Woodstock, VT   05091
(802) 457-2779

Brooks Bird Club
707 Warwood Avenue
Wheeling, WV   26003
(303) 547-5253

The Canvasback Society
Box 101
Gates Mills, OH   44040
(216) 443-2340

Cooper Ornithological Society
Department of Zoology
University of California
Los Angeles, CA 90025

Defenders of Wildlife
1244 19th Street, NW
Washington, DC   20036
(202) 659-9510

Ducks Unlimited
One Waterfowl Way
Long Grove, IL   60047
(312) 438-4300

The Eagle Foundation
300 East Hickory Street
Apple River, IL   61001
(815) 594-2259

Friends of the Earth
530 Seventh Street SE
Washington, DC   20003
(202) 543-4312

George Miksch Sutton Avian Research Center
Box 2007
Bartlesville, OK   74005
(918) 336-7778

Hawk Migration Association of North America
c/o Diann MacRae
22622 53 Avenue SE
Bothell, WA   98021
(206) 481-1797

Hawk Mountain Sanctuary Association
RD 2
Kempton, PA   19529
(215) 756-6961

The Hawk Trust
c/o Birds of Prey Section
London Zoo
Regent's Park, London NW1 4RY
England

International Council for Bird Preservation
219C Huntingdon Road
Cambridge, England CB3 0DL
US section:
Kimberly Young
National Audubon Society
801 Pennsylvania Avenue SE
Washington, DC   20003
(202) 547-9009

International Crane Federation
E-11376 Shady Lane Road
Baraboo, WI   53913
(608) 356-9462

The International Osprey Foundation
Box 250
Sanibel, FL 33957
(813) 472 5218

International Wild Waterfowl Association
217 Ridge Trail
Bozeman, MT   59715

National Flyway Council
c/o Jack Wayland
Washington Department of Game
600 North Capitol Way
Olympia, WA 98504
(206) 753-5710

The National Wild Turkey Federation
Wild Turkey Building
Box 530
Edgefield, SC   29824
(803) 637-3106

National Wildlife Federation
1412 Sixteenth Street NW
Washington, DC   20036
(202) 797-6800

National Wildlife Refuge Association
Box 124
Winona, MN   55987
(507) 454-5940

The Nature Conservancy
1815 North Lynn Street
Arlington, VA   22209
(703) 841-5300

North American Bluebird Society
Box 6295
Silver Spring, MD   20906-0295
(301) 384-2798

North American Loon Fund
RR 4, Box 240C
Meredith, NH   03253
(603) 279-6163

Pacific Seabird Group
Box 321
Bolinas, CA   94924
(405) 868-1434

The Peregrine Fund
World Center for Birds of Prey
5666 West Flying Hawk Lane
Boise, ID   83709
(208) 362-3716

Prairie Grouse Technical Council
University of Minnesota
Natural Resources Department
Crookston, MN   56716

The Purple Martin Conservation
   Association
Box 178
Edinboro, PA   16412

Quail Unlimited
Box 10041
Augusta, GA   30903
(803) 637-5731

Raptor Education Foundation
21901 East Hampden Avenue
Aurora, CO   80013
(303) 680-8500

Raptor Research Foundation
c/o Dr. Jim Fraser
Department of Fish and Wildlife Science
VPI & SU
Blacksburg, VA   24061
(703) 961-6064

The Raptor Trust
2390 White Bridge Road
Millington, NJ   07946
(201) 647-2353

RARE Center for Tropical Bird
   Conservation
19th and the Parkway
Philadelphia, PA   19103
(215) 299-1182

Roger Tory Peterson Institute
110 Marvin Parkway
Jamestown, NY   14701
(716) 665-BIRD

The Ruffed Grouse Society
1400 Lee Drive
Coraopolis, PA   15108
(412) 262-4044

Sierra Club
730 Polk Street
San Francisco, CA   94109
(415) 776-2211

Society for the Preservation of Birds
   of Prey
Box 891
Pacific Palisades, CA   90272

The Trumpeter Swan Society
3800 County Road 24
Maple Plain, MN   55359
(612) 476-4663

Vermont Institute of Natural
   Science
Woodstock, VT   05091
(802) 457-2779

Whooping Crane Conservation
   Association
3000 Meadowlark Drive
Sierra Vista, AZ   85635

Wild Bird Feeding Institute
1441 Shermer Road
Northbrook, IL   60062
(312) 272-0135

The Wilderness Society
1400 Eye Street, NW
Washington, DC 20005
(202) 842-3400

Wildfowl Foundation
2111 Jefferson Davis Highway
Arlington, VA   22202
(703) 979-2626

Wildlife Preservation Trust
   International
34th Street and Girard Avenue
Philadelphia, PA   19104
(215) 222-3636

Wilson Ornithological Society
c/o The Museum of Zoology
The University of Michigan
Ann Arbor, MI   48109
(313) 764-0457

World Pheasant Association of USA
752 Swede Gulch Road
Golden, CO   80401
(303) 526-9270

World Wildlife Fund
1255 23rd Street NW
Washington, DC   20037
(202) 293-4800

Independent Audubon Societies

A number of states have independent Audubon societies not affiliated with the National Audubon Society. This confusing situation dates back to the start of the Audubon movement at the turn of the century, when numerous conservation organizations sprang up using the Audubon name. Many eventually coalesced into what is now the National Audubon Society, but some remained unaffiliated as state societies with their own local chapters, magazines, sanctuaries and activities. To complicate matters further, the National Audubon Society has chapters in every state, including those with independent Audubons. Fortunately, peaceful coexistence and frequent cooperation seem to be the rule.

Connecticut Audubon Society
2325 Burr Street
Fairfield, CT   06430
(203) 259-6305

Florida Audubon Society
1101 Audubon Way
Maitland, FL   32751
(305) 647-2615

Hawaii Audubon Society
Box 22832
Honolulu, HI   96822

Illinois Audubon Society
Box 608
Wayne, IL   60184
(312) 584-6290

Indiana Audubon Society
  Mary Gray Bird Sanctuary
RR 6
Connersville, IN   47331
(317) 825-9788

Maine Audubon Society
Gilsland Farm
118 US Route 1
Falmouth, ME   04105
(207) 781-2330

Audubon Naturalist Society
8940 Jones Mill Road
Chevy Chase, MD   20815
(301) 652-9188

Massachusetts Audubon Society
South Great Road
Lincoln, MA   01773
(617) 259-9500

Michigan Audubon Society
409 West East Avenue
Kalamazoo, MI   49007
(616) 344-8648

Audubon Society of New Hampshire
3 Silk Farm Road
Box 528-B
Concord, NH   03302
(603) 224-9909

New Jersey Audubon Society
Box 125
Franklin Lakes, NJ   07417
(201) 891-1211

State Birding Organizations

Almost every state has a birding association and local bird clubs in addition to the state and local chapters of the National Audubon Society. These organizations generally have local chapters throughout the state. The parent organization and the local groups sponsor meetings, talks, slide shows, newsletters, field trips, bird walks and the like.

Connecticut Ornithological Association
314 Unquowa Road
Fairfield, CT   06430

Denver Field Ornithologists
Denver Museum of Natural History
Denver, CO   80205

Delmarva Ornithological Society
Box 4247
Greenville, DE   19807

Grouse chicks in the nest. A grouse clutch generally has six to twelve eggs.

The Ruffed Grouse Society works to preserve this beautiful bird. Here a male grouse drums to attract a mate.

Federation of New York State Bird Clubs
c/o Constance Wilkins
400 West Road
Cortland, NY   13045

Iowa Ornithologists Union
825 Seventh Avenue
Iowa City, IA   52240

Kansas Ornithological Society
c/o Jane Hershberger
18 Circle Drive
Newton, KS   67114

The Maryland Ornithological Society
Cylburn Mansion
4915 Greenspring Avenue
Baltimore, MD   21209

Minnesota Ornithologists' Union
James Ford Bell Museum of Natural
   History
10 Church Street SE
University of Minnesota
Minneapolis, MN   55455

Nebraska Ornithologists' Union
University of Nebraska State Museum
Lincoln, NE   68508

Oklahoma Ornithological Society
c/o Albert Harris
Route 7, Box 62
Tahlequah, OK   74464

South Dakota Ornithologists' Union
c/o Jocelyn Lee Baker
3220 Kirkwood Drive
Rapid City, SD   57702

Tennessee Ornithological Society
Box 402
Norris, TN   37828

Wisconsin Society for Ornithology
c/o John H. Idzikowski
2558 South Delaware
Milwaukee, WI   53207

GREAT BIRDERS IN AMERICAN HISTORY

America has produced two men who are probably the most famous birders ever: John James Audubon and Roger Tory Peterson. But there were American birders before Audubon, and between the times of Audubon and Peterson are several very influential figures.

Mark Catesby

Mark Catesby (c. 1679-1749) came to Virginia in 1712 and stayed for seven years, sending plant specimens back to England. He returned to England and then came back to America in 1722, where he spent the next four years traveling through South Carolina, Georgia, Florida and the Bahamas. He returned to England for good in 1726 and began work on the illustrations for his famous book *The Natural History of Carolina, Florida and the Bahama Islands*. The first volume appeared in 1731, the second in 1743, and an appendix in 1748. The book had more than 200 illustrations etched by Catesby from his own paintings. His work remained the best study of American birds until Audubon's work a century later.

Alexander Wilson

Alexander Wilson (1766-1813) spent many years in Scotland and America working as a weaver, peddler and schoolteacher before finding his vocation as an ornithologist in 1802. While working as a schoolteacher near Philadelphia, he was befriended by the naturalist William Bartram and encouraged to study and draw the birds. Wilson never learned the art of etching, and hired Alexander Lawson to prepare etchings from his drawings. The first volume of *American Ornithology* appeared in 1808, with seven more volumes appearing by 1813. The excellent introductory essays and informative illustrations make this work outstanding and useful even today, although it covers only the eastern region north of Florida.

John James Audubon

The colorful life of John James Audubon (1785-1851) is the subject of much myth, but the truth is fascinating enough. Audubon was the son of a successful French trader (in slaves, among other things) and a Creole woman. Raised in comfort in France, Audubon came to America in 1803 and settled on his father's estate outside Philadelphia, where he led the life of a country gentleman and first began to study and draw birds. In 1807 he and a friend decided to open a general store in the new lands of Kentucky. In 1808 he married Lucy Bakewell and took her to Louisville with him. Business was less than booming, however, and Audubon had plenty of time to work on his bird paintings even as he and his family moved throughout the Ohio River region in search of a living. Finally, in 1819, bankruptcy ended Audubon's business career. In 1820, the idea of making the birds of America his life's work occurred to Audubon. The

A flamingo from Mark Catesby's *A Natural History of Carolina, Florida and the Bahama Islands*, which appeared in 1731.

This engraving from Alexander Wilson's *American Ornithology* (1808) shows a wood ibis, scarlet ibis, flamingo and white ibis.

John James Audubon, seated at a roadside with his gun. This engraving is taken from the famous portrait of Audubon by Alonso Chappell.

The common American crow, engraved from the painting by Audubon by J.T. Bowen for the Philadelphia octavo edition of *Birds of America*, first published in 1840.

family ended up in New Orleans, where the long-suffering Mrs. Audubon supported the family by teaching. In 1826, after encountering opposition to his work in America, Audubon went to Europe, where he sold subscriptions to his proposed *Birds of America* and was well received. Here he reached an agreement with Robert Havell of London to prepare the engravings for the book from Audubon's paintings.

The elephant folio first edition of *Birds of America* first appeared in parts starting in 1827; the parts continued to appear until 1838. The American octavo edition, with plates prepared by J.T. Bowen, began appearing in 1840; there have been numerous editions since then. In 1842 Audubon moved to his estate on New York State's Hudson River, where he settled down to an enjoyable life as an honored naturalist and artist until his death in 1851.

Thomas Nuttall

Thomas Nuttall (1786-1859) is famed as an ornithologist, but he saw himself primarily as a botanist. Nuttall was born in England and came to America in 1808. He immediately began to travel widely throughout the country collecting plant specimens, work that earned him his reputation as a scientist. In 1822 he became curator of the botanical garden at Harvard, a position he held for ten years. In 1832 he published the trailblazing book *A Manual of the Ornithology of the United States and Canada.* Among other things, this book was the first attempt to reproduce bird sounds through the syllabic method. In addition, it was accessible, well written, accurate and inexpensive. Its low price, at a time when the only other books on the subject were expensive folios by Catesby and Audubon, helped to make the book extremely popular. The first bird club in America, the Nuttall Ornithological Society, was named for him. The club, headquartered at Harvard, still exists; only professional ornithologists are invited to join.

Spencer Fullerton Baird

Few individuals have had as much influence on the science of ornithology as Spencer Fullerton Baird (1823-1887). As a youth of twenty Baird was a friend of Audubon. In 1850 he joined the staff of the Smithsonian Institution, where he rose to become its head. Baird enlisted the aid of U.S. Army surgeons stationed in the West to gather bird specimens and information. Combined with his own work, this data became the basis for Baird's book *The Birds of North America,* the first comprehensive, scientifically arranged checklist of American birds. In addition to his extensive contributions to ornithology, Baird obtained the funds to build the National Museum of Natural History, became the first commissioner of the U.S. Bureau of Fish and Fisheries and founded the Woods Hole oceanic laboratory.

Spencer Fullerton Baird, a guiding light of the Smithsonian Institution and one of America's greatest ornithologists.

Elliott Coues

One of the army surgeons recruited by Spencer Baird, Elliott Coues (1842-1899) went on to a brilliant career in ornithology. Coues did much of his work in the West, as secretary and naturalist for the U.S. Canada Border Commission and for the Geological and Geographical Survey of the Territories. He was a founder of the American Ornithologists' Union; his checklist of North American birds, prepared in 1882, was the basis for the AOU's seminal publication. In all, Coues published nearly a thousand works, including the important *Key to North American Birds.* Coues was an

The dynamic Elliot Coues was a founder of the American Ornithological Union.

outstanding writer and a dynamic, if somewhat eccentric, character. In his later life he was an ardent follower of the spiritualist Madame Blavatsky, at least until he published a paper detailing her fraudulent practices and was expelled from the cult.

Frank Chapman

The man who originated the concept of Christmas bird counts, Frank Chapman (1864-1945) was curator of birds at the American Museum of Natural History for fifty-four years. His contributions as a scientist, educator and conservationist were enormous. Chapman's *Handbook of Birds of Eastern North America* was for many years the standard field guide.

Louis Agassiz Fuertes

By his own account, Louis Agassiz Fuertes (1874-1927) was committed to a career of painting birds by the time he was fourteen. Fuertes grew up near Ithaca, New York, and attended Cornell University. He traveled widely throughout the world in search of birds, and was a skillful, accurate and vibrant artist. His work illustrated numerous bird books published between 1896 and 1927, when he died in a tragic car accident.

Ludlow Griscom

Prior to the influential work of Ludlow Griscom (1890-1959), birding often involved shooting specimens for study. Griscom's achievement was to persuade birdwatchers that careful observation in the field was a superior method to slaughter. Through his extensive writings, brilliance as a speaker and many protégés, Griscom had an important role in transforming birdwatching into the delightful and popular sport it is today.

One of the best bird artists ever was Louis Agassiz Fuertes.

Several organizations, including the International Osprey Foundation, the Raptor Trust, the Raptor Education Foundation and the Raptor Research Foundation are involved with osprey preservation.

Members of The Nature Conservancy enjoy an outing near Orlando, Florida.

FIELD GUIDES AND OTHER READING

A good field guide is as crucial to birding success as good binoculars. What makes a field guide good is a subject for endless discussion among birders. Paintings versus photographs is a hotly debated question; so is organization. There are no definitive answers, and in fact most birders use at least two different general field guides in addition to more specific regional field guides.

The Peterson System

Roger Tory Peterson, the most famous and most honored birdwatcher of this century, revolutionized birding with the publication of his book, *A Field Guide to the Birds,* in 1933. In this volume, illustrated with his own paintings, Peterson presented his system of identifying the birds by their field marks. Each description and painting points out the characteristic features of the species that make it unique—a concept that was a radical change from all other field guides up to that time. Today Peterson's basic concept of field marks is used by all guides.

Basic Field Guides

John Bull and John Farrand, Jr., *The Audubon Society Field Guide to North American Birds,* eastern edition (New York: Knopf, 1977).

Hal H. Harrison, *A Field Guide to Birds' Nests in the Eastern U.S.* (Boston: Houghton Mifflin, 1975).

Hal H. Harrison, *A Field Guide to Birds' Nests in the Western U.S.* (Boston: Houghton Mifflin, 1979).

National Geographic Society Field Guide to the Birds of North America (Washington, DC: National Geographic Society, 1983).

Roger Tory Peterson, *A Field Guide to the Birds,* eastern and western editions, 4th revised edition (Boston: Houghton Mifflin, 1980).

Chandler S. Robbins, Bertel Bruun, Herbert S. Zim and Arthur Singer, *Birds of North America,* expanded and revised edition (New York: Golden Press, 1983).

Miklos D.F. Udvardy, *The Audubon Society Field Guide to North American Birds,* western edition (New York: Knopf, 1977).

Reference Works

A.O.U. Committee on Classification and Nomenclature, *The A.O.U. Checklist of North American Birds,* 6th edition (Washington, DC: American Ornithologists' Union, 1983).

Arthur Cleveland Bent, *Life Histories of North American Birds* (Mineola, New York: Dover Publications, 1962-64).

John Bull, editor, *Simon & Schuster's Guide to Birds of the World* (New York: Simon & Schuster, 1987).

Campbell and Lack, editors, *A Dictionary of Birds* (Vermillion, SC: Buteo Books, 1985).

Ernest A. Choate, *The Dictionary of American Bird Names* (Boston: Harvard Common Press, 1985).

David DeSante and Peter Pyle, *Distributional Checklist of North American Birds* (Artemisia Press, 1986).

John Farrand, Jr., editor, *Audubon Society Master Guide to Birding* (New York: Knopf, 1983).

John Farrand, Jr., *How to Identify Birds* (New York: McGraw-Hill, 1987).

Stephen Kress, *The Audubon Society Handbook for Birders* (New York: Scribners, 1980).

Christopher Leahy, *The Birdwatcher's Companion* (New York: Crown, 1984).

Perrins and Middleton, editors, *The Encyclopedia of Birds* (New York: Facts on File, 1985).

Roger Tory Peterson, *How to Know the Birds* (Boston: Houghton Mifflin, 1957).

John K. Terres, *The Audubon Society Encyclopedia of North American Birds* (New York: Knopf, 1980).

Robert and Esther Tyrrell, *Hummingbirds: Their Life and Behavior* (New York: Crown, 1985).

Alexander Wetmore, *Song and Garden Birds of North America* (Washington, DC: National Geographic Society, 1964).

Information and Entertainment

John James Audubon, *Birds of America* (New York: Abbeville Press, 1987).

Birds: Their Life, Their Ways, Their World (New York: Readers Digest Books, 1980).

John Burroughs, *John James Audubon* (New York: Overlook Press, 1987).

Patricia Caulfield, *Photographing Wildlife* (New York: Amphoto, 1988).

Jack Connor, *The Complete Birder: A Guide to Better Birding* (Boston: Houghton Mifflin, 1988).

Edward W. Cronin, Jr., *Getting Started in Bird Watching* (Boston: Houghton Mifflin, 1986).

Pete Dunne, *Tales of a Low-Rent Birder* (New York: Simon & Schuster, 1986).

Paul R. Ehrlich, David S. Dobkin and Darryl Wheye, *Birder's Handbook* (New York: Simon & Schuster, 1988).

Alan Feduccia, editor, *Catesby's Birds of Colonial America* (Chapel Hill: University of North Carolina Press, 1985).

Erma J. Fisk, *The Peacocks of Baboquivari* (New York: Norton, 1983).

Peter Goodfellow, *Shakespeare's Birds* (New York: Overlook Press, 1983).

George Laycock, *Bird Watcher's Bible* (New York: Doubleday, 1976).

Edward M. Mair, *A Field Guide to Personal Computers for Bird Watchers and Other Naturalists* (Englewood Cliffs, NJ: Prentice-Hall, 1985).

Bill Oddie, *Gone Birding* (New York: Methuen, 1983).

John Shaw, *The Nature Photographer's Complete Guide to Professional Field Techniques* (New York: Amphoto, 1984).

Dr. Lester L. Short, *The Birdwatcher's Book of Lists,* eastern and western editions (New York: Knopf, 1987).

D.R. Griffin, *Bird Migration* (Mineola, New York: Dover Publications, 1974).

Steven G. Herman, *The Naturalist's Field Journal* (Vermillion, SC: Buteo Books, 1986).

Virginia C. Holmgren, *Bird Walk through the Bible* (Mineola, NY: Dover Publications, 1988).

Joseph Kastner, *A World of Watchers* (New York: Knopf, 1986).

Jack Kligerman, editor, *The Birds of John Burroughs* (New York: Overlook Press, 1988).

Laura O'Biso Socha, *A Bird Watcher's Handbook* (New York: Dodd, Mead, 1987).

James M. Vardaman, *Call Collect, Ask for Birdman: The Record-Breaking Attempt to Sight 700 Species of North American Birds Within One Year* (New York: McGraw-Hill, 1980).

Richard H. Wood, *Wood Notes: A Companion and Guide for Birdwatchers* (Englewood Cliffs, NJ: Prentice-Hall, 1984).

Kevin J. Zimmer, *The Western Bird Watcher* (Englewood Cliffs, NJ: Prentice-Hall, 1985).

Backyard Birding

Ken Burke, editor, *How to Attract Birds* (San Francisco: Ortho Books, 1983).

Irene Cosgrove, *My Recipes Are for the Birds* (New York: Doubleday, 1976).

John V. Dennis, *A Complete Guide to Bird Feeding* (New York: Knopf, 1975).

George H. Harrison, *The Backyard Bird Watcher* (New York: Simon & Schuster, 1979).

Stephen W. Kress, *The Audubon Society Guide to Attracting Birds* (New York: Scribners, 1985).

Dr. Noble Proctor, *Garden Birds* (Emmaus, PA: Rodale, 1986).

Donald and Lillian Stokes, *The Bird Feeder Book* (Boston: Little, Brown, 1987).

Donald and Lillian Stokes, *A Guide to Bird Behavior,* volume 1 (Boston: Little, Brown, 1975).

Donald and Lillian Stokes, *A Guide to Bird Behavior,* volume 2 (Boston: Little, Brown, 1983).

Donald and Lillian Stokes, *A Guide to Bird Behavior,* volume 3 (Boston: Little, Brown, 1988).

John K. Terres, *Songbirds in Your Garden* (New York: Hawthorn Books, 1977).

J.L. Wade, *Attracting Purple Martins* (Griggsville, IL: The Nature Society, 1987).

Bird Finding

Peter Alden and John Gooders, *Finding Birds Around the World* (Boston: Houghton Mifflin, 1981).

Herman Heinzel, Richard Fitter and John Parslow, *The Collins Guide to the Birds of Britain and Europe with North Africa and the Middle East* (New York: Stephen Greene Press, 1988).

Roger Tory Peterson with George and Kit Harrison, *Roger Tory Peterson's Dozen Birding Hot Spots* (New York: Simon and Schuster, 1980).

Olin Sewall Pettingill, Jr., *A Guide to Bird Finding,* volumes 1 and 2 (New York: Oxford University Press, 1981).

BOOKSTORES FOR BIRDERS

Any reasonably well-stocked bookstore will carry a few of the most popular American field guides and books about birding, but for anything beyond that a specialist may be needed. Listed below are some reliable mail-order sources of current titles and out-of-print and antiquarian books.

Amaranth Books
Box 527
Iowa City, IA   52240

American Birding Association Books
Box 6599
Colorado Springs, CO   80934
(800) 634-7736

Audubon Naturalist
8940 Jones Mills Road
Chevy Chase, MD   20815
(301) 652-9188

Avian Publications
236 Country Club Lane
Altoona, WI   54720
(715) 835-6806

Buteo Books
Box 481
Vermillion, SD   57069
(605) 624-4343

The Crow's Nest Bookshop
Cornell Laboratory of Ornithology
159 Sapsucker Woods Road
Ithaca, NY   14850
(607) 255-5057

K. Gregory
222 East 71 Street
New York, NY   10021
(212) 288-2119

Houston Audubon Society
The Chickadee Bookstore
440 Wilchester
Houston, TX   77079
(713) 932-1408

HWK Books
540 West 114 Street
New York, NY   10025
(212) 865-6201

John Johnson, Natural History Books
RD 1, Box 513
North Bennington, VT   05257
(802) 442-6738

Doug Kibbe
Box 34
Maryland, NY   12116

Patricia Ledlie
Box 90
Buckfield, ME   04220
(207) 336-2969

Los Angeles Audubon Bookstore
7377 Santa Monica Boulevard
Los Angeles, CA   90046
(213) 876-0202

Marcher's Books
6204 North Vermont
Oklahoma City, OK   73112

Massachusetts Audubon Bookstore
Great Road
Lincoln, MA   01773
(617) 259-9807

National Audubon Society
950 Third Avenue
New York, NY   10022
(212) 832-3200

Orphic Books
18533 Roscoe Boulevard
Suite 200
Northridge, CA   91324

Peacock Books
Box 2024
Littleton, MA   01460

Petersen Book Co.
Box 966
Davenport, IA   52805
(319) 355-7051

Raptor Books
Box 3004
Seattle, WA   98114
(206) 328-5175

Russ's Natural History Books, Inc.
Box 1089
Lake Helen, FL   32741
(904) 228-3356

An excellent source of both current and out-of-print bird books in England is:

Henry Sotheran Ltd.
2-5 Sackville Street
London W1X 2DP

Birding Book Clubs

Birding Book Society
Box 1999
382 Main Street
Salem, NH   03079

The Natural Science Book Club
Riverside, NJ   08075

A water turkey (anhinga) from Visuals.

PERIODICALS

Many bird magazines, newsletters and journals are published. Some, like *The Auk* (the journal of the American Ornithologists' Union), publish scientific papers that are too technical to be of interest to the average reader. Others, like *Audubon*, cover many natural history topics, including birds. The major periodicals of interest are listed below.

General Natural History

Animal Kingdom
New York Zoological Society
The Zoological Park
Bronx, NY   10460
(212) 220-5100
6 times a year; $10.95/year

Audubon
National Audubon Society
950 Third Avenue
New York, NY   10022
(212) 832-3200
6 times a year; $30/year includes
    membership in National Audubon
    Society.

Natural History
American Museum of Natural History
Central Park West at 79th Street
New York, NY   10024
Monthly; $20/year; includes membership
    in museum.

Sierra
Sierra Club
730 Polk Street
San Francisco, CA   94109
6 times a year/$12/year

Wilderness
The Wilderness Society
1400 Eye Street NW
Washington, DC   20005
(202) 842-3400
Quarterly; $30/year; includes membership
    in society.

Birding Magazines

American Birds
National Audubon Society
950 Third Avenue
New York, NY   10022
(212) 832-3200
5 times/year; subscription $27.50/year

The Auk
American Ornithologists' Union
c/o Division of Birds
National Museum of Natural History
Washington, DC   20560
Quarterly; $35/year; includes membership
    in organization.

Birder's World
720 East 8 Street
Holland, MI   49423
(616) 396-5618
6 times/year; $25/year

Birding
American Birding Association
Box 4335
Austin, TX   78765
6 times/year; subscription $28/year for
    nonmembers, included in membership
    dues.

Bird Watcher's Digest
Box 110
Marietta, OH   45750
(800) 421-9764
6 times/year; subscription $15/year

The Living Bird
Laboratory of Ornithology
Cornell University
159 Sapsucker Woods Road
Ithaca, NY   14850
(607) 254-BIRD
Quarterly; $30/year; includes membership
    in Laboratory of Ornithology.

WildBird Magazine
Box 57900
Los Angeles, CA   90057
(213) 385-2222
Monthly; subscription $27/year

Newsletters

The Bird Watch
Bird Populations Institute
Box 637
Manhattan, KS   66502
(913) 238-2887
10 times/year; $10/year; includes
    membership in Bird Populations
    Institute.

ICF Bugle
International Crane Foundation
E-11376 Shady Lane Road
Baraboo, WI   53913
(608) 356-9462
Quarterly; $30/year; includes membership
    in foundation.

Nature Society News
Purple Martin Junction
Griggsville, IL   62340
Monthly; $11/year; includes membership
    in The Nature Society.

BIRD RECORDINGS AND VIDEOS

Although none have gone platinum yet, there are a number of popular recordings of bird songs. Listening to these is an excellent way to learn how to identify birds by their sounds. Some recordings are designed to be used in conjunction with specific field guides. Many of the recordings originate in the Library of Natural Sounds at Cornell's Laboratory of Ornithology (see page 72), although they have different publishers. Those featuring Roger Tory Peterson are put out by Houghton Mifflin. The famous series of recordings by Donald Borror is available from:

Dover Publications
31 East 2 Street
Mineola, NY 11501

Several interesting recordings are available from Droll Yankees in Rhode Island (see page 60).

Instructional video tapes are a relatively new development, with more appearing every month. Several featuring Roger Tory Peterson are produced by Houghton Mifflin. The Audubon Society's video guide to the birds of North America and Ducks Unlimited's guide to waterfowl are produced by Mastervision.

Videos and tapes are usually purchased through a retail outlet (Dover Publishing and Droll Yankees are exceptions). The Crow's Nest Bookshop at Cornell has by far the widest selection of recordings and videos, although other bookshops also carry a good assortment (see page 84). An additional source for tapes and videos is:

NorthWord Inc.
Box 128
Ashland, WI 54806
(800) 336-5666

Also of interest is an unusual recording titled *Symphony of the Birds.* This three-movement musical composition was produced using only sounds made by such common birds as cardinals, robins, song sparrows, Carolina wrens and others. An informative introduction explains the technique and identifies the birds. The other side of the tape is called *Revelations in Bird Song Patterns.* Here the songs of common birds are played at reduced speed. This has the effect of bringing the intricacies of the songs into normal human hearing range. Listening to this tape is indeed a revelation of how complex bird song is. For more information, contact:

Quality Productions
Box 47
Orangeburg, NY 10962
(914) 359-5328

BIRD SLIDES

One of the best ways to learn to recognize birds is to study pictures of them. Slide shows are often presented by bird clubs for this purpose. The pictures often come from the private collections of individual members, but some commercial sources are available. The sources listed below will provide high-quality duplicate slides for private and educational use *only*; these slides may not be reproduced. Write for catalogs.

Cornell Laboratory of Ornithology
Division of Visual Services
159 Sapsucker Woods Road
Ithaca, NY 14850
(607) 254-2450
The laboratory has over 1,000 slides offered at the very reasonable price of $1.40 each. Slide sets (gulls and terns, for example) are available, as are integrated sound/slide sets. Visual Services will also prepare customized slide sets for organizations and individuals.

Maslowski Wildlife Productions
1219 Eversole
Cincinnati, OH 45230
(513) 231-7301
This firm specializes in sharp close-ups. Over 200 slides are available. Slides are $2 each; the minimum order is ten.

VIREO
Academy of Natural Sciences
19th and The Parkway
Philadelphia, PA 19103
(215) 299-1069
Over 100,000 slides are in this massive collection, the largest in the world. Slide sets on such topics as North American raptors, owls and bird families are available. Individual slides are $3 each, with a minimum order of five.

Visuals
Box 381848
Miami, FL 33138
(305) 681-5379
Visuals has hundreds of individual bird slides from around the world. The slides are $2 each; the minimum order is ten.

State Birds

Alabama	*northern flicker*
Alaska	*willow ptarmigan*
Arizona	*cactus wren*
Arkansas	*northern mockingbird*
California	*California quail*
Colorado	*lark bunting*
Connecticut	*American robin*
Delaware	*blue hen chicken*
District of Columbia	*wood thrush*
Florida	*northern mockingbird*
Georgia	*brown thrasher*
Hawaii	*nene*
Idaho	*mountain bluebird*
Illinois	*northern cardinal*
Indiana	*northern cardinal*
Iowa	*American goldfinch*
Kansas	*western meadowlark*
Kentucky	*northern cardinal*
Louisiana	*brown pelican*
Maine	*black-capped chickadee*
Maryland	*northern ("Baltimore") oriole*
Massachusetts	*black-capped chickadee*
Michigan	*American robin*
Minnesota	*common loon*
Mississippi	*northern mockingbird*
Missouri	*eastern bluebird*
Montana	*western meadowlark*
Nebraska	*western meadowlark*
Nevada	*mountain bluebird*
New Hampshire	*purple finch*
New Jersey	*American goldfinch*
New Mexico	*greater roadrunner*
New York	*eastern bluebird*
North Carolina	*northern cardinal*
North Dakota	*western meadowlark*
Ohio	*northern cardinal*
Oklahoma	*scissor-tailed flycatcher*
Oregon	*western meadowlark*
Pennsylvania	*ruffed grouse*
Rhode Island	*Rhode Island red chicken*
South Carolina	*Carolina wren*
South Dakota	*ring-necked pheasant*
Tennessee	*northern mockingbird*
Texas	*northern mockingbird*
Utah	*California gull*
Vermont	*hermit thrush*
Virginia	*northern cardinal*
Washington	*American goldfinch*
West Virginia	*northern cardinal*
Wisconsin	*American robin*
Wyoming	*western meadowlark*

BIRDING HOTLINES

The first rare-bird alert, the Voice of Audubon, was begun in 1954 by the Massachusetts Audubon Society. Today many National Audubon Society local chapters and other birding organizations have birding hotlines—recorded messages announcing where to find rare and unusual birds reported in the locality. The messages are changed at least once a week and often more frequently. The information is often quite detailed; have pen and paper handy to write down notes and directions.

The North American Rare Bird Alert (NARBA) is a commercial service providing information about sightings of unusual birds in North America. The number to hear the recorded message is given only to subscribers. For more information, contact:

Bob-O-Link, Inc.
Box 1161
Jamestown, NC 27282
(800) 438-7539/
In Canada, (800) 438-6704

NEW ENGLAND

Connecticut	(203) 254-3665
Rhode Island	(401) 231-5728
Western Massachusetts	(413) 569-6926
Eastern Massachusetts	(617) 259-8805
New Hampshire	(603) 224-9900
Vermont	(802) 457-2779
Maine	(207) 781-2332

NORTH ATLANTIC STATES

New York City	(212) 832-6523
Albany and Schenectady, NY	(518) 377-9600
Buffalo, NY	(716) 896-1271
New Jersey	(201) 766-2661
Cape May, NJ	(609) 884-2626
Philadelphia, PA	(215) 567-2473
Western Pennsylvania	(412) 963-0560
Wilkes-Barre, PA	(717) 825-2473
Maryland, DC, Delaware and Virginia	(301) 652-1088

MIDWESTERN STATES

Cleveland, OH	(216) 289-2473
Columbus, OH	(614) 221-9736
Toledo, OH	(419) 877-5003
Dayton, OH	(513) 277-6446
Youngstown, OH	(216) 742-6661
Michigan	(616) 471-4919
Detroit, MI and Windsor, ON	(313) 592-1811
Chicago, IL	(312) 671-1522
Central Illionis	(217) 785-1083
Mnneapolis, MN	(612) 544-5016
Duluth, MN	(218) 525-5952
Wisconsin	(414) 352-3857
Iowa	(319) 524-3569
Missouri	(314) 445-9115
Kansas City, MO	(816) 795-8177

SOUTHERN STATES

North and South Carolina	(704) 332-6094
Florida	(305) 644-0190
Alabama	(205) 987-2730
New Orleans, LA	(504) 246-2473
Tennessee	(615) 356-7636
Virginia	(703) 898-3713

WESTERN STATES

Kansas	(316) 343-7061
Texas (statewide)	
from Houston and out-of-state	(713) 747-8826
from Texas	(800) 282-2473
Ft. Worth, TX	(817) 237-3209
Texas Coast	(713) 821-2846
Rio Grande Valley, TX	(512) 565-6773
Austin, TX	(512) 451-3308
San Antonio, TX	(512) 733-8306
Tucson, AZ	(602) 798-1005
Denver, CO	(303) 423-5582
Utah	(801) 530-1299
Wyoming	(307) 265-2473

CALIFORNIA

San Diego	(619) 435-6761
Los Angeles	(213) 874-1318
San Bernardino	(714) 793-5599
Modesto	(209) 571-0246
Santa Barbara	(805) 964-8240
South Sierra	(209) 782-1237
Morro Bay	(805) 528-7182
Monterey	(408) 375-9122
San Francisco (weekly)	(415) 528-0288
San Francisco (daily updates)	(415) 524-5592
Sacramento	(916) 481-0118
Arcata	(805) 658-6094

PACIFIC NORTHWEST STATES

Portland, OR	(503) 292-0661
Seattle, WA	(206) 526-8266
Anchorage, AK	(907) 248-2473

CANADA

Alberta	(403) 237-8821
Victoria, BC	(604) 592-3381
Vancouver, BC	(604) 876-9690
Windsor, ON and Detroit, MI	(313) 592-1811
Windsor & Pt. Pelee, ON	(519) 252-2473
Ottawa, ON	(613) 596-4888
Eastern Quebec (in French)	(819) 778-0737

4
ART FOR
BIRD LOVERS

Bird Art • Magazines for Art Lovers • Wildlife Art Museums • Bird Art Publishers • Wildlife Art Galleries • Bibelots for Birders

BIRD ART

Artists have been fascinated by the elusive beauty of birds for thousands of years, from cave artists and the ancient Egyptians to the present. It is only since the emergence of ornithology as a science in the middle of the sixteenth century that accurate (and incidentally beautiful) bird illustration emerged. By the nineteenth century—and the age of John James Audubon—bird art was becoming an art form in itself, the birds being depicted simply for their own beauty. This trend gathered force and continues very strongly into this century. An astonishing number of outstanding artists have chosen birds as their life work. Names such as Owen Gromme, Roger Tory Peterson,

The tenth anniversary Michigan duck stamp print by Bob Steiner, available from Steiner Prints.

Bob Steiner did the 1987 fifth anniversary New Hampshire duck stamp print, published by Steiner Prints.

Hasty Departure, a carving of Eastern Shore black ducks by J.D. Sprankle, one of the finest waterfowl carvers working today.

George Miksch Sutton, Sir Peter Scott, Robert Bateman, Maynard Reece and Guy Coheleach are just some of this century's artists widely recognized by the art-loving public.

Interest in wildlife and bird art continues to grow rapidly. Duck stamp prints, limited edition prints and other art are in demand; new museums open and older museums mount wildlife art exhibits. In part this strong interest may represent a nostalgic wish to capture the vanishing natural world that few can see in person anymore. Mostly, it is that many wildlife artists, no matter what their medium, combine accuracy and vision in a way that is very beautiful.

Prints

By far the most collectible area of bird art is limited-edition prints reproduced from original paintings. These prints are signed and numbered; after the edition is sold out, the printing plates are destroyed and the print is available only on the secondary market. Fine prints fall into two basic categories.

Duck stamp prints. In 1934 the financial base of the National Wildlife Refuge system was laid by passage of the Migratory Bird Hunting Stamp Act. This law requires all waterfowl hunters to purchase an annual migratory bird stamp, or "duck" stamp, in order to hunt on federal lands. The money collected in this way goes to support and enlarge the refuge system. In 1934, the first stamp was issued from a quick design executed by J.N. "Ding" Darling, head of the U.S. Biological Survey (ancestor of today's U.S. Fish and Wildlife Service). From 1935 to 1949, artists were invited to execute the stamp painting. In 1950, the first open national de-

An antique wooden decoy from the extensive collection at the Shelburne Museum.

sign competition was held; eighty-eight pieces were entered. By 1988, the number of entries had jumped to over 2,000. The original painting chosen for each year's stamp is used to make the stamp design. The artist receives a small payment, but also has the valuable right to issue a limited-edition print of the painting.

The duck stamp was adopted by many states, again as a way to raise money for state wildlife refuges. States issuing duck stamps include Alabama, Alaska, Idaho, Indiana, Minnesota, New York, Oklahoma, Virginia and West Virginia.
Other limited-edition prints. Limited-edition prints of bird subjects are issued by many fine-art publishers. These prints are creating by making a color separation from the original painting, using a complex photographic process. The separations are used to make printing plates, and the prints are run off on a special press. The process is complicated and lengthy, and anything less than a perfect reproduction, faithful in color and detail, is rejected. A print issue is generally announced in advance to allow collectors to subscribe. Some editions are limited by number. That is, the number of prints in the issue is fixed in advance and run off; the printing plates are then destroyed so that no further prints can ever be made. Less often, an edition is limited by time. That is, subscriptions are taken for a fixed period of time. When the time limit expires, only the number of subscriptions ordered is printed. Again, the plates are destroyed. In either case, the artist signs and numbers each print.

In the process of making the prints numerous test proofs are pulled, often under the artist's supervision. Sometimes the artist will make comments in the margin. Prints carrying such comments, or remarques, are sometimes sold; these are usually signed but not numbered, since technically they are not part of the limited edition.

When purchasing a print, the paper used to make it is an important consideration. The best prints are made on acid-free rag paper using fade-resistant inks. The seller should be able to tell you the year the print was published, the name of the artist and publisher, how many prints were in the regular edition and how many additional prints were retained by the artist and publisher (for donation to a conservation group, for example). The number retained should not exceed 10 percent of the total edition. Obviously, the more famous the artist and the smaller and scarcer the edition, the more value the limited-edition print is likely to have.

Wood Carvings

Wood carvings of wildfowl, either as decorative pieces or as decoys, are becoming increasingly popular. Antique decoys are fetching ever-higher prices, while a thriving community of contemporary artists turns out one beautiful piece after another. In addition, many amateur artists are turning to carving wildfowl and other birds.

When buying an antique decoy, look for good condition and an assurance of authenticity. Most antique decoys were carved to be used and may show signs of a hard and active life. This is not necessarily undesirable; however, indications of wood worms or rot are. Sadly, because antique decoys were meant to be functional, their simple designs are sometimes copied by modern workers who then artificially distress the wood and fade the paint to give an antique appearance. Buy your wood carving from a reputable dealer. The many bird carving exhibits, shows and demonstrations held every year are a good place to learn about antiques, carving techniques, artists and dealers.

This cardinal family is made by Titan Art Glass.

Barn Swallow by Neil Blackwell, released by Artwell Publishing.

Sound of Wings by Manfred Schatz, represented by the Russell A. Fink Gallery.

MAGAZINES FOR ART LOVERS

There are several informative, illustrated magazines for those interested in wildlife art.

Southwest Art
CBH Publishing Inc.
Box 460535
Houston, TX   77056
(713) 850-0990
Monthly; $27.50/year

Wildfowl Carving & Collecting
Box 1831
Harrisburg, PA   17105
(717) 234-5091
Quarterly; $29.95/year

Wildlife Art News
3455 Dakota Avenue South
St. Louis Park, MN   55416
(612) 927-9056
6 times a year; $24/year

WILDLIFE ART MUSEUMS

Some fascinating museums are devoted to wildlife art of various sorts, including bird art.

Academy of Natural Sciences
19th and The Parkway
Philadelphia, PA   19103
(215) 299-1000
Admission: free
A number of bird artists are well represented here. The collection includes 225 watercolors by Louis Agassiz Fuertes as well as works by Audubon, Alexander Wilson, John Gould and others.

American Museum of Wildlife Art
Box 10
Frontenac, MN   55026
(612) 345-5295
Admission: free
Founded by the Webster family, owners of Wild Wings Galleries, the American Museum of Wildlife Art has a good collection of original works by a number of well-known artists, as well as a good library. A part of this young museum is devoted to permanent displays by outstanding artists. The first artist to be so honored is the famed Owen Gromme, who has also donated his extensive egg collection to the museum.

James Ford Bell Museum of Natural History
University of Minnesota
10 Church Street, SE
Minneapolis, MN   55455
(612) 642-1852
Admission: $2/adults
The museum has temporary exhibits by contemporary artists.

Ray Harris-Ching made the original painting for this print, *Winter Wren*, published by the Russell A. Fink Gallery.

Genessee Country Museum
Gallery of Sporting Art
Box 1819
Rochester, NY 14603
(716) 538-6822
Admission: $7/adults
Founded in 1976, this large gallery has one of the largest collections of wildlife and sporting art in the country—over 700 pieces. Of particular interest to bird lovers is the Audubon/Tunnicliffe gallery, featuring works by these artists and others.

National Museum of Natural History
10th and Constitution Avenue, NW
Washington, DC 20560
(202) 357-3129
Admission: free
The museum does not have a permanent collection of wildlife art, but it does sponsor exhibitions such as the extremely popular Robert Bateman exhibit held in 1987.

New-York Historical Society
John J. Audubon Gallery
170 Central Park West
New York, NY 10024
(212) 873-3400
Admission: $2/adults
The New-York Historical Society owns 433 of the 435 lifesize watercolor paintings done by Audubon as the basis for the Havell engravings for his Birds of America *(the other two have been lost). A group of between sixty and 100 is exhibited on the fourth floor; the selection is changed periodically.*

North American Wildfowl Art Museum of the Ward Foundation
655 South Salisbury Boulevard
Salisbury, MD 21801
(301) 742-4988
Admission: $2/adults
Some 2,000 antique decoys and modern bird sculptures fill this amazing museum. The Ward Foundation has been sponsoring the annual World Championship Wildfowl Carving Competition since 1971.

Noyes Museum
Lily Lake Road
Oceanville, NJ 08231
(609) 652-8848
Admission: $1.50/adults
The decoy collection at this museum includes over 500 pieces, many from New Jersey. Decoy carving demonstrations are held.

San Bernadino County Museum
2024 Orange Tree Lane
Redlands, CA 92374
(714) 792-1334
Admission: free
The Wilson C. Hanna ornithology collection, which includes many fine bird specimens and over 40,000 eggs, is housed in this museum. The museum sponsors the annual Wildlife West Festival.

Shelburne Museum
Shelburne, VT 05482
(802) 985-3344
Admission: $10/adults
The extensive collection of folk art at the Shelburne Museum includes numerous bird decoys and carvings. A fascinating collection of carved eagles is also on display, as are many bird and wildlife paintings and prints.

Wildlife World Art Museum
18725 Monument Hill Road
Monument, CO 80312
(303) 488-2460
Admission: $3/adults
This museum claims the world's largest collection of bird carvings, with over 2,200 works by 125 different artists. Original paintings by many well-known artists, including some 100 canvases by Gary Cobeleach, are on exhibit, along with many bronzes.

Leigh Yawkey Woodson Art Museum
Franklin and 12 Street
Wausau, WI 54401
(715) 845-7010
Admission: free
The Woodson Art Museum is widely acknowledged as the best of its kind in the country. Founded in 1973, it launched the first of its now-famous annual Birds in Art exhibits in 1976. This exhibit features the finest in bird art by the most outstanding artists. The exhibit is shown at the museum and then goes on national (and sometimes international) tour. The permanent collection of paintings, bronzes and carvings at the museum is excellent. Among the artists collected are Robert Bateman, Gary Cobeleach, Sir Peter Scott and Bruno Liljefors.

Prints by Belgian artist Carl Brenders are published by Mill Pond Press. This work is called *White Elegance—Trumpeter Swans.*

The masterful paintings of Canadian artist Robert Bateman are issued in print form by Mill Pond Press. Shown here is *Tawny Owl in Beech*.

May Brings Flowers, by Liz Lesperance, is published by Voyageur Art.

BIRD ART PUBLISHERS

The companies listed below publish original, signed, limited-edition prints by major artists for the primary market.

American Masters Foundation
10688 Haddington, Suite 200
Houston, TX   77043

Artwell Publishing
16281 Perdido Key Drive
Pensacola, FL   32507

Cedar Creek Publishers
2712 Mallard Court
Columbia, MO 65201

Chukar Press
Box 943
Walla Walla, WA   99362

Russell A. Fink Gallery
Box 250
Mason Neck
Lorton, VA   22079

Gray Stone Press
205 Louise Avenue
Nashville, TN   37203

The Greenwich Workshop
30 Lindeman Drive
Trumbull, CT   06611

Hadley House
14200 23 Avenue North
Plymouth, MN   55447

Mill Pond Press
310 Center Court
Venice, FL   34292

Mountain Wilderness Press
22528 Blue Jay Road
Morrison, CO   80465

Nature's World in Print
Box 132
Elkins, WV   26241

Northwoods Craftsman
4144 Briar Ridge Lane
Colgate, WI   53017

Pacific Wildlife Galleries
3420 Mt. Diablo Boulevard
Lafayette, CA   94549

Pawnee Creek Press, Ltd.
Box 633
Cedar Rapids, IA   52406

Petersen Prints
6275 Sunset Boulevard, Suite 429
Los Angeles, CA   90028

Premier Art Editions Ltd.
100 West Beaver Creek Road, Unit 10
Richmond Hill, Ontario L4B 1H4

Riverview Art
9551 Riverview Road
Eden Prairie, MN   55347

Stanton & Lee
44 East Mifflin Street
Madison, WI   53703

Steiner Prints
201 Fifth Avenue, Suite 8
San Francisco, CA   94118

Terfli Higgins Publishing Company
3500 Route 97
Glenwood, MD   21738

Voyageur Art
2828 Anthony Lane South
Minneapolis, MN   55418

Wild Wings
Lake City, MN   55041

Willow Creek
Box 300
Wautoma, WI   54982

Individual Artists

Ted Blaylock
Blaylock Originals
1152 East 8 Place
Mesa, AZ   85203

Lisabeth Clapham
LeLac
532 Elizabeth
Rochester, MI   48063

Bill Hunt
Rebecca Carpenter-Hunt
7177 Langley Court
Salinas, CA   93907

James Landenberger
Pawnee Creek Press Ltd.
Box 633
Cedar Rapids, IA   52406

Bruce Matteson
Matteson Studio
South Haven, MI   49090

Catherine McClung
Box 43
Dexter, MI   48130

J.D. Sprankle
Route 2, Box 731-B
Chester, MD   21619

Bob Steiner
Steiner Prints
201 Fifth Avenue, Suite 8
San Francisco, CA   94118

Michael Van Houzen
115 East Crapo
Alpena, MI   49707

One of the greatest bird painters of this century is New Zealander Ray Harris-Ching. This print, published by the Russell A. Fink Gallery, is titled *Early Snow—Mourning Doves*.

WILDLIFE ART GALLERIES

The galleries listed below deal primarily in mail-order sales of limited-edition prints by various artists; they do not publish prints. They sell art on both the primary and secondary markets.

Audubon Prints and Books
9720 Spring Ridge Lane
Vienna, VA 22180
(703) 759-5567

Black Duck Gallery
555 Thames Street
Newport, RI 02840
(401) 846-0150

Cardinal Art Gallery
Box 1189
Vernon, NJ 07462
(201) 764-5050

Carlson Images, Inc.
109 Brandywine Place
Lansing, MI 48906
(517) 372-1118

Charles River Prints, Inc.
36 Riverside Drive
Waltham, MA 02154
(617) 893-7974

The Decoy Den
107 East Main Street
St. Charles, IL 60174
(312) 584-0330

Delaware Sporting Gallery
100 South Delaware Avenue
Seaford, DE 19973
(302) 629-4666

Four Seasons Gallery
Box 2174
Jackson, WY 83001
(307) 733-4049

Gallery Jamel
White Plains Commerce Center
White Plains, MD 20695
(301) 870-2457

Gallery One
7003 Center Street
Mentor, OH 44060
(800) 621-1141

Gallery 247
816 Merrick Road
Baldwin, NY 11510
(516) 868-4800

G&R Gallery of Wildlife Art
2895 Seneca Street
Buffalo, NY 14224
(716) 822-0546

GWS Galleries
26390 Carmel Rancho Lane
Carmel, CA 93923
(800) 843-6467/(408) 625-2288

Mader's
1037-41 North Third Street
Milwaukee, WI 53203
(800) 558-7171

Manor Wildlife Gallery
2780 Bristol Pike
Bensalem, PA 19020
(215) 245-4922

Marlton Gallery
2 North Maple Avenue
Marlton, NJ 08053
(800) 524-1061/(609) 983-3771

Maverick Arts
417 Northeast Couch Street
Portland, OR 97232
(800) 346-3006

National Wildlife Galleries
Box 06497
Fort Myers, FL 33906
(800) DUCK ART

Nature's Gallery
121 Ghent Road
Akron, OH 44313

Pacific Wildlife Galleries
3420 Mt. Diablo Boulevard
Lafayette, CA 94549
(415) 283-2977

Pleasonton Wildlife Art
800 Main Street
Pleasonton, CA 94566
(415) 846-1824

Starkweather Alley Gallery
215 North Main Street
Romeo, MI 48605
(313) 752-5859

Susquehanna Decoy Shop
Kitchen Kettle Village
Intercourse, PA 17534
(717) 768-3092

Sutter Buttes Wildlife Gallery
4013 B Colusa Highway
Yuba City, CA 95991

Western Visions
408 Broad Street
Nevada City, CA 95959
(800) 422-6239/(916) 265-6239

Wildlife of the World Gallery
521 East Hyman Avenue
Aspen, CO 81611
(303) 925-6800

Wild Wings Galleries
Lake City, MN 55041
(800) 445-4833/(612) 345-5355

Wild Wings Galleries was begun by William B. Webster in 1968. Today, in addition to an extensive mail-order operation, there are twenty retail locations carrying many exclusive fine art prints and other beautiful gift items. The Webster family founded the American Museum of Wildlife Art in Frontenac, Minnesota. Since 1973 the company and the artists it represents have jointly donated limited-edition prints to nonprofit conservation organizations for use in fund-raising. The many Wild Wings outlets cannot all be listed here. However, one gallery stands out for the excellent wood carvers it represents:

Wild Wings Decoy Den
Bell Tower Shops
13499 US 41, SE
Fort Myers, FL 33907
(813) 482-8585

Barn Swallows on Fence Post, by well-known Canadian artist Ron Parker, is published by Mill Pond Press.

The best-known contemporary bird artist in the world may well be Roger Tory Peterson. This print, published by Mill Pond Press, is called *Puffins*.

Maynard Reece is best known for his waterfowl and game bird paintings. This print, *Oak Timber—Mallards,* is published by Mill Pond Press.

Kentucky Warbler by Fenwick Lansdowne from the Greenwich Workshop in Trumbull, Connecticut.

The winner of the 1988 federal duck stamp contest and of many other contests is Daniel Smith. Voyageur Art published this print, titled *Winter Sentinel*.

This print of hummingbirds is by James Landenberger.

BIBELOTS FOR BIRDERS

From T-shirts to tote bags, tie pins to thermometers, if something can have a bird on it, it probably does. The mail-order sources listed below carry items that range from the practical to the frivolous. Whether you buy them as gifts, conversation pieces or for real use, the birds will help you enjoy them more.

Mail Order Catalogs

Crow's Nest Bookshop
Cornell Laboratory of Ornithology
159 Sapsucker Woods Road
Ithaca, NY   14850

Duncraft
Penacook, NH   03303

The Nature Company
Box 2310
Berkeley, CA   94702

Owl's Nest
Box 5491
Fresno, CA   93755

Bumper Stickers

Bird Life
2445 Vincente Street
San Francisco, CA   94116

Carving Supplies and Tools

Buck Run Carving Supplies
151 Gully Road
Aurora, NY   13206

CraftWoods
10921A York Road
Hunt Valley, MD   21030

P. C. English Inc.
Box 380
Thornburg, VA   22565

Clocks

Merry Clocks
2239 Poinsettia Drive
San Diego, CA   92106

Cushions

The Thimbleberry
22365 Wooster Road
Danville, OH   43014

Games

Birding Trivia
Quail Inc.
Box 314
Thief River Falls, MN   56701

A selection of mobiles from Skyflight Mobiles.

Glass and Stained Glass

Glasscraft Inc.
626 Moss Street
Golden, CO   80401

Titan Art Glass
4651 Mt. Comfort Road
Fayetteville, AR   72701

Utopia Glass
Route 1
Park Falls, WI   54552

Jewelry

The 14 Karat Parrot
Box 182
Sanibel Island, FL   33957

Vern Wayne Pond
Studio 3
105 North Union Street
Alexandria, VA   22314

Whispering Pines Studio
2215 Crumarine
Moscow, ID   83843

Willard Jones
Box 1537
Green Island, NY   12183

Mobiles

Bird Alert
Route 3, Box 120
Cedarcreek, MO   65627

Skyflight Mobiles
Box 3393
Bellevue, WA   98009

Needlepoint Kits

Abacus, Ink.
Box 1081
Marietta, OH   45750

Postage Stamps

George Ford
Box 5203
Gulfport, FL   33737

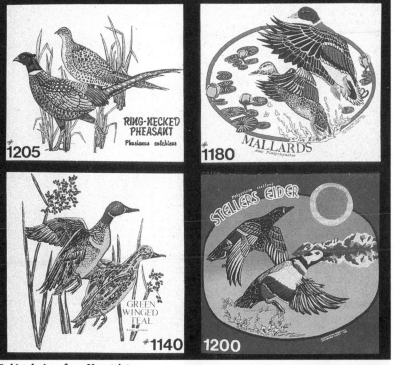

T-shirt designs from Mountaintop.

A flock of bird pillows made by **Thimbleberry**.

Slate-Colored Junco, carved by Michigan artist Michael Van Houzen.

Beth Erlund works in batik to create bird paintings on fabric. This print of a ruby-throated hummingbird is titled *Springtime*; it is published by Mountain View Press.

This suction-cup window thermometer is made by Aspects.

Aspects makes these large patio thermometers.

A female northern cardinal basks in the sun in this photo from Carlson Images.

T-Shirts

Robert Engel
Box 308
Oak View, CA   93022

Feathers 'n Fabrics
Box 2764
Escondido, CA   92025

Friends of a Feather
167 Atlantic Avenue
Long Branch, NJ   07740

Gliding Gull Studio
130 Cherry Street
Box 293
Whitelaw, WI   54247

Make Tracks!
3253 Warick
Royal Oaks, MI   48702

Jim Morris
Box 831
Boulder, CO   80306

Mountaintop
Eden, VT   05652

Rain Creek Productions
Box 281
Rochester, IN   46975

Ridge Runner Naturals
1033½ Balsam Road
Waynesville, NC   28786

W. Stiles Co.
2375 Derby Street
Troy, MI   48084

Tiles

McCusick Tile
Route 1, Box 35D
Globe, AZ   85501

Tote Bags and Handbags

Cody Co.
Box 32102
Fridley, MN   55432

Mapleleaf Creations
Box 524
Bristol, NH   03222

Windchimes

Patio Pleasers
621 North Fourth Avenue
Tucson, AZ   85705

Vermont comfort birds, made by David Ross, are very soothing to hold.

Silver jewelry handmade by Vern Wayne Pond.

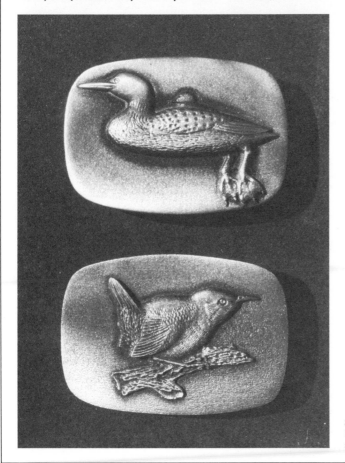

Sid Bell Originals makes pewter belt buckles as well as other bird jewelry in pewter and silver.

Porcelain Birds

When Edward Boehm (1913-1969) opened his studio in Trenton, New Jersey, in 1950, his goal was to create ". . . only true porcelain sculptures that are faithful to nature, perfect in every detail." He achieved this goal so successfully, ably assisted by his wife Helen, that today magnificent Boehm sculptures are found in 121 museums the world over. The exquisite artistry that makes Boehm birds famous is beautifully represented not only in individual pieces but also in the annual Boehm/Audubon series. For more information, contact:

Edward Marshall Boehm, Inc.
25 Fairfacts Street
Trenton, NJ   08638

Other manufacturers of limited-edition collectible porcelain birds include:

The Franklin Mint
Franklin Center, PA   19091

The Hamilton Group
9550 Regency Square Boulevard
Jacksonville, FL   32232

Lenox Collections
One Lenox Center
Langhorne, PA 19092

Bald Eagle is the first issue in The Hamilton Group's American Birds of Prey sculpture collection.

A cardinal is part of the Lenox Collections' Garden Bird sculpture series.

Robin from Boehm depicts a mother robin in her nest.

Prothonotary Warbler with Daffodils, a porcelain sculpture from Boehm.

The Lenox Collections' Garden Bird sculpture collection includes this blue jay.

This fairy tern from Boehm is the sixth in the annual Boehm/Audubon series.

The Hamilton Group's Majestic Owls of the Night sculpture collection has *Barn Owl* as its first issue.

This black-capped chickadee is one of the sculptures in the Garden Bird
series from Lenox Collections.

The first issue in The Hamilton Group's North American Ducks sculpture collection is
Common Mallard.

Steuben Glass

The master craftsmen of Steuben Glass produce a number of gorgeous bird representations at the Steuben factory in Corning, New York. Some are free-standing crystal or glass sculptures; others are objects such as flasks or bowls. All are produced in very limited editions; all are magnificent. For more information, contact:

Steuben Glass
Fifth Avenue at 56 Street
New York, NY 10022
(212) 752-1441

The wild pheasant and wild quail designs from the Steuben Glass Wild Game Flasks Collection.

This bowl, designed by James Houston, is engraved with a flight of snipe above wind whipped weeds. It is made by the craftsmen of Steuben Glass.

This solid crystal owl is from the Hand Coolers Collection handmade by Steuben Glass.

This blown crystal peacock from Steuben Glass was designed by Bernard X. Wolff.

5
BIRDING HOTSPOTS

North America • Canada • Central and South America • The Caribbean Islands • Europe and the Near East • Africa • Asia • Australia, New Zealand and Papua New Guinea • Tours for Birders

In this chapter the selection of the world's birding hotspots is arranged geographically within each continent, with the exception of Europe where the countries are arranged alphabetically. Information on touring individual countries or regions accompanies each description where applicable and more general travel information is located both at the end of each continent section and at the end of the chapter.

NORTH AMERICA
Alaska

A trip to Alaska in the spring is every birder's dream: magnificent scenery, long, long days for watching and birds seen nowhere else in North America. Alaska is huge—over 586,000 square miles—and empty—only about 520,000 people. Over 47 million acres of the state have been set aside to form fifteen spectacular national parks, and much genuine wilderness remains as a haven for birds and wildlife. Alaska has very long, cold winters and short, warm summers. Warm is a relative term, however, and it is important to bring warm clothing, raingear and good, waterproof shoes or boots even in the prime visiting season from late May through September. Insect repellent is absolutely vital; protective clothing is advisable. Many places in Alaska can be reached only by boat, plane or on foot; always make arrangements in advance. Be prepared for delays and itinerary changes due to inclement weather.

Southeastern Alaska. This region of Alaska includes the panhandle bordering British Columbia and part of the coastal region of the Gulf of Alaska. Birding along the coast is spectacular; the largest concentration of bald eagles in the state is found at Seymour Canal. Glacier Bay National Park is a good place to spot whales. It is also a good place to see horned grebes, western flycatchers, marbled murrelets, fox sparrows, Pacific loons, black-legged kittiwakes, guille-mots, shearwaters, petrels, bald eagles, cormorants, gulls, rock ptarmigans and many other birds. Trumpeter swans nest in the Cooper River drainage at Wrangell-St. Elias National Park, and many migratory birds pass through.

South central Alaska. The spectacular mountain scenery of the Kenai Peninsula and Kenai Fjords National Park and the magnificent Columbia Glacier is almost unbelievably beautiful. Huge colonies of black-legged kittiwakes nest on the cliffs, and murrelets, red-faced cormorants, oystercatchers, horned puffins, three-toed woodpeckers, Steller's jays and Townsend's warblers are just some of the birds seen.

Alaska Peninsula and Aleutian Islands. Truly dedicated birders travel to the windswept, desolate island of Attu, at the very tip of the Aleutian chain, to see the incredible variety of migrating birds and the many unusual vagrants found there. Those who are slightly less dedicated can still find excellent birding in the more accessible Katmai National

An American oystercatcher seen at Kenai Fjords National Park.

A huge flock of rock sandpipers takes to the air near the Kachemak Bay Lodge, not far from Homer, Alaska.

Park and Preserve at the northern end of the peninsula. The many lake edges and marshes of the park are nesting areas for red-necked grebes, whistling swans, ducks, loons and arctic terns. Peregrine falcons, bald eagles, hawks and owls nest on the cliffs, seabirds abound along the coast and forty different songbirds summer here. In addition, brown bears, moose and many smaller animals live in the park. The tiny Pribilof Islands of St. Paul and St. George in the Bering Sea, 800 miles (1,300 km) from Anchorage, provide spectacular numbers of seabirds, including eleven different cliff-dwellers. Common and thick-billed murres, tufted and horned puffins, crested, parakeet and least auklets, northern fulmars, red-legged kittiwakes and others are here in incredible abundance. The breeding colony of thick-billed murres is estimated at over one million birds. In addition, more than one million northern fur seals congregate on the shores of the islands each summer.

Northwest Alaska. The birds of the high arctic can be seen in this portion of the state, part of which lies well above the Arctic Circle. The grassy tundra is home to Steller's and spectacled eiders, snowy owls, red phalaropes, jaegers and pectoral sandpipers, among other interesting species. This is midnight sun territory in the summer.

A common murre guards her egg on the rocks at Kachemak Bay.

The Canadian North

The Yukon. The lower portion of the Yukon Territory, including the magnificent Inside Passage, will offer many of the same birds found in southern Alaska. Likewise, the arctic species seen in northeastern Alaska will also be seen in the Yukon. As in Alaska, the best time to visit is between May and September. Be prepared: unpredictable cold spells can happen at the peak of summer. Bring warm clothing and lots of mosquito repellent.

Churchill, Manitoba. Most famous for its annual invasion by migrating polar bears, Churchill is on the west coast of Hudson Bay. The tundra around Churchill is an important resting point for birds heading toward the Arctic. Vast numbers of red phalaropes, gulls (including Ross's gulls), jaegers, whimbrels and other migrants are present in the spring. Harlequin ducks, black guillemots and fifteen different shorebirds breed in the region; other birds include short-eared owls, orange-crowned warblers, hoary redpolls and others.

Black-legged kittiwakes nest in incredible numbers on the cliffs of the Alaska coast.

Beautiful ptarmigans are seen in the Canadian Yukon.

A harlequin duck displays its camouflage while swimming in Kachemak Bay.

Gull Island in Kachemak Bay, with the Kenai Mountains in the background.

Visiting the Far North

Organized group tours of Alaska and the Canadian North are available from many operators, but it is also fairly easy to make your own arrangements and hire a private guide. This route is not for the faint of heart, however, since it often involves wilderness canoeing and hiking. Below is a list of guides and lodges.

Alaska
Goose Cove Lodge
Box 325
Cordova, AK   99574
(907) 424-5111

Kachemak Bay Wilderness Lodge
China Poot Bay via Box 956
Homer, AK   99603
(907) 235-8910

Wilderness Birding Adventures
Box 10-3747
Anchorage, AK   99510

Canadian North
Arctic Waterways
RR 2
Stevensville, Ontario L0S 1S0
(416) 382-3882

Bathurst Inlet Lodge
1 Boffa Drive
Box 820
Yellowknife, Northwest Territories X1A
   2T2
(403) 873-2595

Canoe Arctic Inc.
Box 130
Fort Smith, Northwest Territories X0E
   0P0
(403) 872-2308

Churchill Wilderness Encounter
Box 9
Churchill, Manitoba   R0B 0E0
(204) 675-2248/(204) 222-7877

East Wind Arctic Tours
Box 2728
Yellowknife, Northwest Territories X1A
   2R1
(403) 873-2170

Oldsquaw Lodge
Bag Service 2711
Whitehorse, Yukon Territory Y1A 4K8

Primrose Wilderness Encounters
Box 4775
Whitehorse, Yukon Territory Y1A 4N6
(403) 668-3881

Riding Mountain Nature Tours
Box 429
Erickson, Manitoba R0J 0P0
(204) 848-2977

Yukon Expeditions
127 Alsek Road
Whitehorse, Yukon Territory Y1A 3K7
(403) 667-7960

A tern chick on New Brunswick's Machias Seal Island.

Watching snow geese at the Oak Hammock Marsh in Manitoba.

The Pacific Northwest

Washington, Oregon and northern California all offer impressive coastlines, mountains and birds. The bird populations usually hit their peaks in August, when the weather is also good. This region is a good place to see bald eagles, falcons and ospreys, many species of shorebirds and many other birds.

California. Redwood National Park, stretching along the coast of Humboldt Bay north of Eureka to just south of the Oregon border, preserves groves of massive redwood trees. The Pacific flyway brings over 300 species through the park. Peregrine falcons, avocets, redknots, phalaropes, bald eagles, brown pelicans, Aleutian Canada geese, gulls, terns, spotted owls, American dippers, black oystercatchers, ruffed grouse, tufted puffins and wrentits are just some of the birds found here.

Oregon. Malheur National Wildlife Refuge, in the dry scrublands of eastern Oregon, is a good site for migrating waterbirds and other western birds. Trumpeter swans, sandhill cranes and sage grouse are common; other frequently seen birds include golden eagles, long-billed curlews, Wilson's phalaropes, Say's phoebes, canyon wrens, white-faced ibises and white pelicans. The region around Upper Klamath Lake in southern Oregon, near the California border, is famed for migrating waterbirds. The Klamath Basin National Wildlife Refuges in the area offer good birding. Refuges in this system include Bear Valley, Clear Lake (in California), Klamath Forest, Lower Klamath (partly in California), Tule Lake (in California) and Upper Klamath.

Washington. The northern Cascade Mountains and the Columbia River are excellent birding sites with a wide range of habitats. The subalpine ridges are excellent for observing raptor migration: northern harriers, sharp-shinned hawks, Cooper's hawks, rough-legged hawks, golden eagles and kestrels can all be seen. North Cascades National Park contains an estimated 200 bird species. The Skagit River in the park is excellent for winter sightings of common mergansers, Barrow's goldeneyes, common goldeneyes and bald eagles feeding on salmon. The head of Lake Chelan is a nesting area for Canada geese, soras, yellowthroats and other wetland birds. Ross Lake is on the migration corridor; birds breeding there include ospreys, loons, grebes, white-winged scoters, sandhill cranes and terns.

These Atlantic puffins winter in the North Atlantic. Horned and tufted puffins are found on the Pacific coast.

A ptarmigan shows its winter white near Churchill, Manitoba.

Every summer the Alf Hole Sanctuary near Rennie, Manitoba, is home to a flock of some 200 giant Canada geese.

A loon at South One Lake in Manitoba. Loons leave the water only to nest.

California

Over 500 species can be seen in California, an indication of the state's wide geographical diversity. California has the highest mountain in the continental United States—Mt. Whitney, 14,494 feet (4,350 m)—and the lowest point in America—Death Valley, 282 feet (85 m) below sea level. The Monterey Bay is fantastically rich in seabirds, as are other regions of the coast; many excellent pelagic tours are available. In contrast, within the same state is Yosemite National Park in the High Sierras, offering many montane birds.

Coastline birding. Several areas of the California coast are particularly good for pelagic birds. The San Diego region is famous for rare and vagrant birds, par-

ticularly in the autumn. Birds commonly seen include cormorants, many gulls, Pacific loons, brown pelicans, ruddy turnstones and sanderlings. The Point Loma area offers many passerines, including yellow-rumped warblers, Anna's hummingbirds, hermit thrushes, wrentits and others. Monterey Bay south of San Francisco is extraordinarily rich in birds. Among the many that can be seen are murres, jaegers, shearwaters, gulls, terns, black-footed albatrosses and auklets. An added bonus is the presence of several whale species. Point Reyes National Seashore north of San Francisco has murres, ducks, egrets, herons, grebes, loons, terns, sandpipers, cormorants, guillemots and phalaropes, among others—more than 200 species

can be seen here on a good day. This is also a good site for vagrants, especially in the fall.

High Sierra and Yosemite. The rugged mountains of the High Sierra Nevada range provide some incomparable birdwatching, especially in the late summer. White-headed woodpeckers, Cassin's finches, American dippers, blue grouse, great gray owls, black-backed woodpeckers, pine grosbeaks, numerous warblers and many more montane species can be seen. The east slope of the High Sierras drops off sharply and leads to the Great Basin desert. Here the brine shrimp that breed in saline Mono Lake attract eared grebes, California gulls, red-necked phalaropes and Wilson's phalaropes, among others.

A murre colony at Point Reyes National Seashore, north of San Francisco.

Columns of volcanic rhyolite tower over the scenery at Chiricahua National Monument, Arizona.

Gulls and terns along Gold Bluffs Beach at Redwood National Park in northern California.

The stunning scenery on Pebble Beach at Crescent City, part of Redwood National Park, is as interesting as the gulls.

The ponderosa pine forest in Totem Canyon at Chiricahua National Monument is a good place to see many interesting Mexican birds, including the coppery-tailed trogon.

Southern California and Arizona Deserts

The low-lying desert areas of the southwest offer fascinating winter birding.

Salton Sea. The Salton Sea in the Imperial Valley is part of the Colorado River that has been caught in a desert sink. It attracts large numbers of wintering waterbirds, and vagrants are often seen. Birds that can be seen there include mountain plovers, burrowing owls, mountain bluebirds, yellow-footed gulls and white-faced ibises.

Anza Borrego Desert. This barren area, often compared to a moonscape, supports a surprising variety of bird life, including California quails, Anna's hummingbirds, Costa's hummingbirds, wrentits, black-tailed gnatcatchers, California thrashers, black-throated sparrows and tricolored blackbirds.

Joshua Tree National Monument. Lying partly in the high-elevation Mojave Desert and partly in the lower-elevation Colorado Desert, Joshua Tree National Monument also has palm oases and several water impoundments, most notably Barker Dam. Over 200 species have been documented in the half million acres of the park. Birds commonly seen include burrowing owls, golden eagles, roadrunners, hummingbirds and wrens; many desert sparrows are also found. Joshua Tree National Monument is best visited from November to April; in the summer months temperatures over 100°F (38°C) are not infrequent.

Big Morongo Preserve. Some 100 miles north of Los Angeles is Big Morongo Preserve, a 3,900-acre desert oasis that attracts many migrating songbirds, including vermilion and brown-crested flycatchers.

Arizona

Few hotspots anywhere can match the varied terrain of southeastern Arizona—summer or winter. The best times to see breeding birds are May, July and August; the winter months offer good weather and winter migrants. In northern Arizona are the awesome Grand Canyon and many desert oases that attract a wide variety of birds.

Saguaro National Monument. Located outside of Tucson, the monument preserves a section of the Sonoran Desert with a superb stand of the giant saguaro cactus. Within the park the elevation changes some 6,500 feet (1,950 m), leading to a great diversity of plant and animal life. Birds to be seen include curve-billed thrashers, cactus wrens, Gambel's quails, Gila woodpeckers, Mexican juncos, Mexican jays, Steller's jays and rufous-sided towhees. A trip here in April will probably have the extra bonus of a spectacular display of blooming plants.

Patagonia area. South of Tucson, the Patagonia region is the location of the Nature Conservancy's Patagonia-Sonoita Creek Sanctuary. This riparian woodland harbors over 250 species, including gray hawks, rose-throated becards, flycatchers, kingbirds, phoebes and many more. Many Mexican birds are found here, and a wide variety of warblers pass through in the spring and fall migrations. The Mile Hi reserve at nearby Ramsey Canyon is also operated by the Nature Conservancy. The hummingbirds here are attracted by feeders; as many as ten species may be seen.

Chiricahua Mountains. The Chiricahua Mountains are a world apart from the Sonoran and Chihuahuan deserts that surround them. In these cool, moist "sky islands" are found many of the plants and animals typical of the Southwest, and also many found in the Sierra Madre of Mexico. Among the many species of birds that can be seen here are sulphur-bellied flycatchers, Mexican chickadees, acorn woodpeckers, coppery-tailed trogons, warblers, hummingbirds and owls. What makes Chiricahua such a mecca for birders is the wide range of habitats found within its 11,134 acres (4,454 ha). These include grassland, interior chapparal, Madrean evergreen wood-land, riparian deciduous forest, montane coniferous forest, cliffs and riparian scrub. Elevations range from low desert to coniferous forest at a level of 9,000 feet (2,700 m).

Grand Canyon. September and October are good months for birding at the Grand Canyon and vicinity. Resident birds to be seen then include pygmy nuthatches, mountain bluebirds, black-chinned sparrows and Cassin's finches.

Pipe Spring National Monument. This historic complex, built by Mormon

Jaunty-looking roadrunners can be seen at Big Bend National Park.

settlers, is a well-known oasis for migrating birds. Numerous flycatchers and warblers can be seen, as well as green-tailed towhees and other birds.

Texas

Texas is a huge state with a tremendous range of habitats; it's no wonder it attracts birders from all over the world. In the Rio Grande valley are numerous Mexican birds, while east Texas is famed for the migrating birds that pass through in late April and early May on their way north from the tropics. The southern coast of Texas is also the summer home of the whooping crane. In the hill country of the western part of the sate is Big Bend National Park, the only American home of the Lucifer hummingbird and Colima warbler.

Upper coast. Millions of birds pass over the portion of the Texas coast northeast of Houston every spring on their way north. On occasion weather conditions (especially north winds) will cause massive fallouts of birds in migrant traps in the area around High Island. When this happens, up to twenty-five different warblers can be seen; tanagers, buntings, orioles, flycatchers and others are also found. In this area are the famous Bolivar flats, where great numbers of terns, plovers, avocets, gulls and shorebirds can be seen. Anahuac National Wildlife Refuge is a wonderful place to see several types of rails, including yellow and black rails.

Big Thicket National Preserve. Sometimes called "the biological crossroads of America," Big Thicket National Preserve contains a remarkable number of habitats within its 84,850 acres. Over 300 bird species either live in the preserve or migrate through; so diverse is the terrain that eastern bluebirds may nest near roadrunners. Among the birds to be seen here are yellow-billed cuckoos, Louisiana waterthrushes, Bachman's sparrows, hooded warblers and the endangered red-cockaded woodpeckers. Rain, heat and humidity are

Turkey vultures roost on a dead tree in Big Bend National Park in Texas.

Mixed hardwood and pine forest at Big Thicket National Preserve is home to many different bird species.

Sandhill cranes at Padre Island National Seashore.

A black-bellied plover strolls along the shore at Padre Island National Seashore.

part of the Big Thicket experience. Rain can be expected every month of the year; the average yearly rainfall is 55 inches. Daytime temperatures in the summer are often around 90°F (32°C).

Padre Island National Seashore. The barrier islands of Padre Island National Seashore on the southern coast are home to laughing gulls, white pelicans, terns, herons, egrets, sandpipers, killdeers, meadowlarks, sandhill cranes and many waterbirds. In the spring many passerine migrants are found in the area.

Aransas National Wildlife Refuge. The home of the whooping crane from late October to early April, Aransas National Wildlife Refuge is also the home of sandhill cranes, roseate spoonbills, white-faced ibises and many other birds. Ironically, although many birders travel to Aransas to see the whoopers, the birds

On the barrier islands of the Padre Island National Seashore many species of waterfowl, including pintail ducks, can be seen.

are found mostly in an area that is closed to the public. The birds can often be seen from an observation tower and on boat tours, however.

Attwater Prairie Chicken National Wildlife Refuge. This interesting reserve, located near the town of Eagle Lake, is a protected booming ground for greater prairie chickens. The birds can be seen performing their mating ritual at dawn and dusk in the late winter and early spring. However, arrangements to visit must be made in advance.

The Rio Grande Valley. South Texas, particularly along the Rio Grande Valley, offers fantastic birding, including many Mexican species. Falcon Dam, west of Rio Grande City, is a well-known spot for kingfishers, Audubon's orioles, red-billed pigeons and brown jays.

Santa Ana National Wildlife Refuge. At the southern tip of Texas, Santa Ana is a real hotspot, with over 300 species recorded. This is an excellent spot for long-billed thrashers, great kiskadees, Altamira orioles, white-tipped doves, olive sparrows, buff-bellied hummingbirds and many others.

Hill country. The hill country of Texas is known as much for its stunning wildflowers as for its birds. Vermilion flycatchers, golden-cheeked warblers, green kingfishers and cave swallows are among the birds here.

Big Bend National Park. The forested Chisos Mountains in Big Bend National Park rise 8,000 feet (2,400 m) above the desert floor of the Rio Grande valley. The varied ranges provided by the terrain means that a great variety of birds find homes in the park. Among those seen here are many Mexican species; the only American nesting sites of the Colima warbler and Lucifer hummingbird are here. Other birds seen here are gray vireos, varied buntings, zone-tailed hawks, elf owls, hepatic tanagers and black-chinned sparrows.

Caspian and royal terns observe the surf at Padre Island National Seashore.

South Bird Island, one of the barrier islands that make up Padre Island National Seashore, is home to these white pelicans.

The only American nesting sites of the Colima warbler are in Big Bend National Park.

A green heron stalks its prey in Biscayne National Park.

Florida

South Florida is the only tropical region in the United States. As such, it has birds seen nowhere else in the country. It also has mosquitos in quantities unequalled elsewhere—wear protective clothing and bring *lots* of repellent.

Everglades National Park. This incredible (and seriously endangered) national park covers some 1.4 million acres (560,000 ha). The rich and varied animal and bird life is best seen in the winter, when the drier weather forces them to congregate around the waterholes, and when the mosquitos and other insects are not so pesky. At this time the nature trails and roads along the

(west of Homestead) is only half a mile long, but it offers one of the best opportunities to see wildlife close up. Anhingas, herons, egrets and purple gallinules inhabit the area, as do alligators, turtles and marsh rabbits. The Shark Valley road, located 30 miles (48 km) west of Miami on the Tamiami Trail in the slow-moving Shark River Slough, is a 15-mile (24-km) loop passing through the range of snail kites and wood storks, among other birds. Visitors can walk or bike on the road, or take a tram ride. Big Cypress National Preserve, which borders Everglades National Park, covers 570,000 square acres. The bird life is similar.

The Dry Tortugas. A cluster of seven coral reefs almost 70 miles (112 km) west of Key West, the Dry Tortugas are the site of Fort Jefferson National Monument. These waterless islands are an important stopover point for migrating birds on their way to Cuba and South America. One of the greatest wildlife spectacles in the world occurs on tiny Bush Key every year between April and September, when some 100,000 sooty terns and a colony of over 2,500 brown noddies gather for their nesting season. In the summer large numbers of frigatebirds also congregate on the islands, and roseate terns nest on some of the keys. In the migration seasons warblers, thrushes, buntings and other birds pass through in large numbers, and interesting vagrants are often seen. The Dry Tortugas are accessible only by boat or seaplane from Key West; the site has no water or facilities.

Ding Darling National Wildlife Refuge. On the Gulf Coast of Florida near St. Petersburg, the J.N. "Ding" Darling National Wildlife Refuge is located on Sanibel Island, a 12-mile (19-km) barrier island. The refuge is named after one of the pioneers of the conservation movement, Jay Norwood Darling, who headed the U.S. Biological Survey under Franklin Roosevelt. The total area of about 6,500 acres stretches from Sanibel to Tampa Bay. The refuge is an excellent spot for seeing wintering migratory waterfowl such as blue-winged teals, pintails, shovelers, widgeons and coots. Waders such as herons, egrets and ibises are often seen. Other birds found here include brown pelicans, least terns, black skimmers and laughing gulls.

Lake Woodruff National Wildlife Refuge. The famed St. Johns River forms the western boundary of this 18,400-acre migratory bird refuge on the Atlantic coast near Daytona Beach. Approximately 200 species of birds can be seen, including southern bald eagles, ospreys, limpkins, wood storks, sandhill cranes and twenty-one species of ducks in the fall and winter.

Photographer/guide Flip Pallott captured this delightful scene on a salt marsh in the Everglades. Raccoons dash across the marsh in front of egrets and an ibis.

many ponds in the park are good places to see birds. Among those found in the Everglades are roseate spoonbills, ospreys, great white herons, brown pelicans, wood storks, anhingas, sandhill cranes, snail kites, Cape Sable sparrows, Florida mangrove cuckoos, short-tailed hawks and many others. About fifty pairs of southern bald eagles nest along the coast. Two trails in the park are of particular interest to birdwatchers. The Anhinga Trail near the main visitor center

Corkscrew Swamp Sanctuary. To the north of Big Cypress is the well-known Corkscrew Swamp Sanctuary near Naples, owned and operated by the National Audubon Society. The sanctuary contains one of the largest stands of mature bald cypress trees in the nation, including some that are nearly 500 years old. The 1-¾-mile (3-km) boardwalk loop is a good place to see the largest colony of wood storks in the country as well as many wading and other birds.

An endangered peregrine falcon soars above Big Bend National Park in Texas.

Symbolic of Florida, flamingos wade in Biscayne National Park.

Among the many waterbirds at Padre Island are spoonbills.

An osprey surveys the Everglades.

One of the smaller terns, the common tern is often mistaken for a gull. Terns almost always have forked tails; gulls have tails that are squared-off or rounded.

A common egret wades through the marsh at Gulf Islands National Seashore in Florida

White ibises perch on a buttonwood tree in the Everglades.

Photographer Flip Pallott caught this roseate spoonbill on film in the Florida Everglades.

A great blue heron poses at Gulf Islands National Seashore in Florida.

Hawaii

The seven Hawaiian islands have active volcanos and tropical rainforests. The bird life is quite interesting and also quite endangered—thirty-six species are listed by the federal government as threatened or endangered, mostly by habitat destruction. The Nature Conservancy maintains the Kamakou Preserve on the island of Molokai. This 2,774-acre (1,110-ha) tract preserves a piece of the island's rainforest, the habitat for the Hawaiian thrush, the Molokai creeper and three other honeycreepers.

The Maine Coast

The rocky coast of Maine is pocked with inlets, bays and coves, while the offshore waters are dotted with hundreds of islands. The area is spectacularly beautiful in the summer, when the birding is particularly excellent.

Acadia National Park. Mount Desert Island, the highest elevation on the eastern seaboard, is part of Acadia National Park, as are the picturesque Schoodic Peninsula on the mainland and the spectacular cliffs of Isle au Haut. Yellow-bellied flycatchers and Swainson's thrushes are among the songbirds; many seabirds are found in the park as well.

Machias Ship Island. This small island is home to colonies of Atlantic puffins, Arctic terns and razorbills; many other seabirds are found feeding in the waters off the island.

Monhegan Island. The quiet island of Monhegan offshore from Port Clyde is a good spot to see migrating landbirds in the autumn; numerous raptors can also be seen.

New Jersey

The place to bird in New Jersey—indeed in the entire Northeast and possibly the nation—is Cape May, where the southern tip of the state juts into Delaware Bay. The cape is a resting and assembly point for birds making the 18-mile (29-km) flight over the bay, and its location is perfect for funneling birds on the Atlantic flyway through the area. In ad-dition, because strong northwesterly winds sometimes blow southbound birds back inland, the birds may "stack up" on the cape to await better weather. The autumn raptor migration is easily visible here; the passerines and other birds in the spring defy description. The New Jersey Audubon Society runs the Cape May Bird Observatory here; visitors are welcome. (For more information about the observatory, see page 242.) The annual World Series of Birding is held at Cape May every spring. The 187-acre (75-ha) Cape May Migratory Bird Refuge, run by the Nature Conservancy, is here as well.

North Dakota

The central flyway used by migrating waterfowl passes over North Dakota. The broad grasslands of the state offer some outstanding birding.

Long Lake National Wildlife Refuge. This important refuge was established in 1932. It contains 22,310 acres (8,924 ha) located in Burleigh and Kidder counties in the south-central part of the state. Long Lake is quite shallow; at its normal level it covers 16,000 acres (6,400 ha). There are few large trees in the refuge, and consequently few passerines are seen. However, this is compensated for by the large numbers of interesting waterfowl and upland birds. Among those seen here are pintails, mallards, upland plovers, marbled godwits, willets, sandhill cranes, blue-winged teals, and several species of geese. Of particular interest are Baird's sparrows and sharp-tailed sparrows. Migrating whooping cranes can sometimes be seen resting in the refuge. Beginning in late August spectacular concentrations of Franklin's gulls can be seen; waterfowl populations peak in late October, when Long Lake hosts up to 40,000 ducks and 15,000 geese.

Other sites. Arrowwood National Wildlife Refuge near Pingree and Upper Souris National Wildlife Refuge near Minot are good spots for birding. At Upper Souris up to 100,000 waterfowl can be seen during the spring and fall migrations. Baird's, LeConte's and sharp-tailed sparrows can be seen here, as can Sprague's pipits. In addition, there are 148 state wildlife management areas in North Dakota. All are good places to see waterfowl and other birds.

Pennsylvania

Two places in Pennsylvania are outstanding birding hotspots.

Hawk Mountain Sanctuary. This sanctuary may be one of the most famous hot spots in the world. During the fall migration over 10,000 hawks have been seen in a single day.

Presque Isle State Park. During the spring migration numerous passerines stop at this peninsula on southeastern Lake Erie. It has much the same attraction for birds—and many of the same species—as the more famous Point Pelee, Ontario, on the northern shore of the lake (see page 167).

U.S. Information Sources

When planning a birding trip, it's always helpful to have an idea of the birds to be expected as well as where to see them, places to stay, and so on. A good place to start is with the state's National Audubon Society chapter (see pages 67–68). The staff can help with checklists and hot spots and can tell you about any planned field trips and other activities in the area. Contact the state tourism, wildlife and parks offices as well. The tourism office can provide maps, information about lodgings, restaurants and activities; the wildlife office can often provide refuge lists, checklists and other useful information. The parks office can provide information about park activities and campsites. To locate a state tourism office, call directory assistance in the state capital. Ask for the tourism office; if there is no listing, ask for the department of economic development. The wildlife office is generally headquartered in the state capital; ask for the fish and game department and speak with a nongame biologist. The state parks division is also usually based in the state capital; ask for the department of natural resources if there is no listing under the parks department.

Write ahead to any national parks or national wildlife refuges you plan to visit—the rangers, who are uniformly enthusiastic and helpful, can provide checklists and information.

Alaska
Nature Alaska Tours
Dan L. Wetzel
Box 10224
Fairbanks, AK 99710

Attour
2027 Partridge Lane
Highland Park, IL 60035
(312) 831-0207

Florida
Flip Pallott
5555 S.W. 67 Avenue, #107
Miami, FL 33155
(305) 667-3430

Lovett E. Williams
Florida Wildlife Services, Inc.
2201 S.E. 41 Avenue
Gainesville, FL 32601
(904) 371-3142

North Carolina
Paul G. DuMont
750 South Dickerson Street
Arlington, VA 22204
(703) 931-8994

Pacific Coast
Baja Bird Expeditions
2625 Garnet Avenue
San Diego, CA 92109
(800) 843-6967/(619) 581-3311

Pacific Adventures
Box 268
Cotati, CA 94928
(707) 795-8492

Shearwater Journeys
Box 1445
Soquel, CA 95073
(408) 688-1990

Southwest
Rick Bowers
1402 East Manlove #56
Tucson, AZ 85719
(602) 628-8825

North American Tour Companies

North America
Cardinal Birding Tours
Box 7495
Alexandria, VA 22307
(703) 360-4183

Field Guides Incorporated
Box 160723
Austin, TX 78746
(512) 327-4953

Diane Holsinger
Route 1, Box 88
Timberville, VA 22853
(703) 896-7132

Massachusetts Audubon Society
Tour Director, Conservation Department
Lincoln, MA 01773
(617) 259-9500

McHugh Ornithology Tours
101 West Upland Road
Ithaca, NY 14850
(607) 257-7829

Parula Tours
1711 West Oglethorpe Avenue
Albany, GA 31707

Questers
257 Park Avenue South
New York, NY 10010
(212) 673-3120

Raptours
Box 8008
Silver Spring, MD 20907
(301) 565-9196

Victor Emanuel Nature Tours
Box 33008
Austin, TX 78764
(512) 477-5091

Wings
Box 31930
Tucson, AZ 85751
(602) 749-1967

Snow geese are among the many spectacular migrant birds that can be seen at Padre Island National Seashore.

A woodpecker at Big Thicket National Preserve, Texas.

Black skimmers fly just above the waves at Padre Island National Seashore on the Texas coast.

157

Birding in the National Parks

An Act of Congress on March 1, 1872 established Yellowstone National Park in the territories of Wyoming and Montana as ''a public park or pleasuring ground for the benefit and enjoyment of the people'' and placed it ''under exclusive control of the Secretary of the Interior.'' Thus Yellowstone became the cornerstone of a national park system that now comprises 337 different areas across the country. In 1977 the system encompassed only about 31.1 million acres (12.4 million ha). The additions of 47.1 million acres (18.8 million ha) in Alaska under President Jimmy Carter in 1978 more than doubled the total acreage, bringing it to 79 million acres (31.6 million ha). The founding of Yellowstone also began a worldwide national parks movement. Today more than 100 nations support some 1,200 national parks.

The American national park system covers a tremendous range of habitats, from the saltwater wetlands of Acadia National Park in Maine to the arid desert of Death Valley National Monument in California and Nevada. The bird life visible in the parks is correspondingly diverse. All life forms in the national parks are protected by law—take nothing but photographs.

When planning a trip to a national park, it is always best to write ahead for information. A complete index listing all units of the system is available for a very modest fee from the Government Printing Office or from:

Office of Public Affairs
National Park Service
Department of the Interior
Washington, DC   20240
(202) 343-7394

For information about individual parks, write to the information officer, mentioning a specific interest in birdwatching. Expect a prompt response enclosing brochures describing the park and its facilities. In addition, many parks will send along a bird checklist.

When arriving at the park, check in at the visitor center. Many parks have staff naturalists who can fill you in on what birds are in the area and direct you to likely spots. There may also be organized field trips led by rangers with local knowledge. Checklists, other publications and slides will usually be available for purchase as well.

Sadly, as other wilderness areas shrink, the pressures on the national park system increase. This means that there will be crowds of people at the most popular parks at the most popular times. You may find yourself jostling for space for your tripod, and the ranger staff is stretched thin. Advance reservations at campgrounds, motels and the like are a must. The solution to overcrowding has two parts: visit the less famous (but equally fascinating) parks, and go in the fall, winter and spring instead of the summer. You'll see the migrations and winter plumages—and you'll have the place to yourself. Some intriguing parks that are off the beaten path are listed below.

Biscayne National Park
Box 1369
Homestead, FL   33090

Just 21 miles (37 km) east of Everglades National Park and not far from Miami, Biscayne National Park contains 175,000 acres of tropical habitat fringed by keys and coral reefs. The shallow waters of the bay attract waders and waterbirds, including brown pelicans, snowy egrets and a large nesting colony of little blue herons. Pied-billed grebes and red-breasted mergansers winter in the park, and white-crowned pigeons are year-round residents. Boobies and gannets can sometimes be sighted out to sea. In total, 179 species are known to occur in the park. In addition, accidental and pelagic species are not uncommon, adding an extra bit of excitement to birding at Biscayne. The climate at the park is subtropical, with warm, wet summers and mild, dry winters; annual rainfall is about 65 inches (165 cm). Mosquitos and other biting insects are present in abundance year round; always bring repellent.

At Biscayne National Park birdwatchers can sometimes watch ospreys plunge into the water to pursue prey.

Also known as a wood ibis, the wood stork prefers marshy areas like Biscayne National Park.

The royal tern is a winter resident of Biscayne National Park.

A frigatebird circles over Sandwich Island in Biscayne National Park.

Cormorants spread their wings to dry on Black Point Jetty at Biscayne National Park.

160

A white pelican surveys Biscayne National Park from a typical perch—a pier piling.

Canaveral National Seashore
Box 6447
Titusville, FL   32782

Canaveral National Seashore consists of 25 miles (40 km) of undeveloped barrier island that preserves natural beach, dune, marsh and lagoon habitats for many species of birds. The park consists of 57,627 acres (23,050 ha); this includes a portion of the 140,393-acre (56,157 ha) Merritt Island National Wildlife Refuge. Over 300 birds make their home or travel through the Seashore/Refuge, including the bald eagle, wood stork and scrub jay, all endangered species. Because of the diverse collection of wetland habitats, most of the wading birds and other waterfowl for which Florida is famous can be seen at some time in the year. A variety of ranger-led programs, including bird walks, are offered in the New Smyrna Beach area, which is the northern access point for the park. Bird life abounds on Merritt Island. Gulls, terns, sandpipers, herons, egrets, ibises, pelicans and osprey are common; the endangered southern bald eagle, eastern brown pelican and peregrine falcon can also be seen. Because Merritt Island is a key wintering area along the Atlantic flyway, a visit during a migration period will add many birds to your life list. Hunting of migratory waterfowl is permitted during the fall migration. Some sections of the park are sometimes closed because of activity at nearby Kennedy Space Center. When visiting the inland areas of the park away from the effect of offshore breezes, be sure to carry mosquito repellent—you'll need it.

Unlike the more familiar blue jay, the scrub jay, often seen at Canaveral National Seashore, has no crest.

Wading birds converge at a marsh in Canaveral National Seashore.

Wood thrush nestlings are fed by their parents at Mammoth Cave National Park in Kentucky.

Wild turkeys at Mammoth Cave National Park.

Mammoth Cave National Park
Mammoth Cave, KY   42259

Best known for its enormous limestone cave (300 miles [480 km] of passageways and still counting), Mammoth Cave National Park is as interesting above ground as below, at least from a birder's perspective. The 51,000 surface acres became a national park in 1941, at which time the many small farms within the park were abandoned. Over the years the land has reverted to a natural wilderness of hardwood and coniferous forest, attracting more and more birds and wildlife. Today over 200 bird species have been recorded in the park. American redstarts, scarlet tanagers, sixteen nesting warbler species, indigo buntings, wild turkeys, wood thrushes, many woodpecker species and many other land birds. As many as thirty different warblers can be found during the spring migration, especially in the first week of May. An excellent short book, *Birds and Their Habitats in Mammoth Cave National Park;* by Gordon Wilson, is available at the visitor center.

Fire Island National Seashore
120 Laurel Street
Patchogue, NY   11772

Fire Island is a 32-mile (51-km) barrier island separating the Atlantic Ocean from the Great South Bay and the south shore of Long Island. A number of separate summer communities are on the island, but serious efforts have been made to preserve the natural life there. In 1980 a 7-mile (11-km) stretch of the island incorporating about 1,400 acres (560 ha) was designated by Congress as wilderness, the only such area in New York State—and perhaps the only one in the country practically within sight of skyscrapers. The area is reached by ferry between May and November or by private boat year round; once there, access is by foot only. The endangered least tern arrives at the area from South America in April or May and establishes breeding areas on bare sand near the high-tide line. Great numbers of waterbirds rest on the quiet waters of the Great South Bay during the migration periods; many, many birds of all species stop to rest. In summer the park is a good place to see more than fifty kinds of gulls, herons, ducks, shorebirds and common mid-Atlantic songbirds. When birdwatching anywhere on Fire Island beware of poison ivy—to say that it flourishes there is an understatement.

Waterbirds of all sorts are seen at Fire Island National Seashore. Here a male common pintail, a duck usually seen in marshes, swims on serene waters.

Redheads, like the male shown here, prefer bays.

The male common eider is a sea duck.

The unusual bill of the black skimmer is uneven, with the lower part longer than the upper. Skimmers feed by flying just above the water and dipping in the lower bill to catch small fish, crabs and other food.

Sanderlings, shown here in their white winter plumage, feed along the shore at Fire Island National Seashore.

Apostle Islands National Lakeshore
Route 1, Box 4
Bayfield, WI   54814

Twenty picturesque islands and an 11-mile (18-km) strip of Bayfield Peninsula along the south shore of Lake Superior make up this unusual park. Birdwatching in the park's islands is particularly enjoyable because there are no roads or utility lines. Birds are best seen from the islands, not the mainland portion of the park. The islands lie along one of the major flight paths over the Great Lakes, and spectacular numbers of hawks and songbirds can be seen in spring and fall. The south end of Outer Island is particularly good for viewing the fall and spring passerine flights. The beaches of Outer and Stockton islands are good for seeing migrant shorebirds. Gull and Eagle islands contain nesting colonies of gulls, cormorants and herons; during the breeding season boats may not approach closer than 100 yards (90 m). Hawks are scarce during the autumn, and all birds are very scarce in the winter. An excellent and inexpensive guidebook, *Birds of the Apostle Islands* by Stanley A. Temple and James T. Harris, can be purchased at the park.

Grand Teton National Park
Moose, WY   83012

Some 293 bird species have been observed in the 310,521 acres (124,208 ha) of Grand Teton National Park, but the primary bird attraction is the bald eagle population. This magnificent bird, now endangered south of the Canadian border, has one of its last healthy nesting areas in the Greater Yellowstone Ecosystem, including Grand Teton and Yellowstone parks. More than sixty pairs nest in the summer, and about 300 eagles are resident in the winter. The bald eagle is one of the largest birds found in the ecosystem, along with the sandhill crane, whooping crane and trumpeter swan. Eagles in the park should be observed from a distance, especially during critical nesting times, generally February through August. Many eagles are banded. Should you observe a marked bird, note the date, time of day, location, activity, color of the band and the leg it is on and report the information to a ranger. It will be forwarded to the Greater Yellowstone Ecosystem Working Group, which is responsible for implementing an extensive interdepartmental recovery plan for bald eagles. Among the common birds known to nest in the park are the calliope hummingbird, several species of grouse, the belted kingfisher, MacGillivray's warbler and the mountain bluebird. The peak season in Grand Teton is from early June through late September. Extreme conditions in the winter can include nighttime temperatures of -40°F (-40°C) and snow to a depth of 5 feet (1.5 m).

Eagles nest in this tree at Apostle Islands National Lakeshore.

CANADA
Ontario

The province of Ontario has one of the most famous birdwatching places in the world: Point Pelee. It also has numerous other excellent, if little known, sites.

Point Pelee. Point Pelee National Park, the southernmost point on Canada's mainland, occupies the southern half of this 9-mile (14-km) spit of land extending into western Lake Erie. During the spring and fall migrations very large numbers of birds congregate here, either preparing to cross Lake Erie in the fall or resting from the crossing in the spring. The best time to bird on Point Pelee is in May, when the peninsula is crammed with tanagers, flycatchers, warblers, orioles, vireos, grosbeaks, buntings, thrushes and others heading north. Herons, hawks, swallows, gulls and other birds can also be seen. The Boardwalk Trail is a convenient way to see the birds; it extends for two-thirds of a mile into the marsh and leads to an observation tower. Other good birding spots in southwestern Ontario on Lake Erie include Rondeau Provincial Park and Long Point Provincial Park.

Hawk Cliff. Between Point Pelee and Long Point, the Hawk Cliff sanctuary is located on the high, steep clay cliffs on the northern shore of Lake Erie. The site offers a spectacular view of the fall migration, particularly impressive flights of raptors.

Jack Miner's Bird Sanctuary. Just north of Kingston, this world-famous sanctuary is a feeding and marshalling ground for large flights of geese and other waterfowl. The best times to visit in the spring are the last three weeks in March and the first two weeks in April; in the fall, the last ten days of October and first week of November are best. The late afternoon is the best time of day to see the birds in flight.

Pinery Provincial Park. On Lake Huron near Grand Bend, this park features the annual northward migration of tundra swans. Up to 10,000 of these birds can be seen at a time in March, along with many other geese and ducks.

Gaspé Peninsula, Quebec

The Gaspé Peninsula in Quebec contains a famous seabird colony on Bonaventure Island off the coast. Teeming numbers of northern gannets, black-legged kittiwakes, common murres and razorbills can be seen, along with Atlantic puffins. In the woods of the mainland are boreal chickadees, Swainson's thrushes, many species of warblers and finches, gray jays and many others.

Newfoundland and Labrador

Newfoundland and Labrador offer two major seabird sanctuaries. At Cape St. Mary's on the cape shore of Newfoundland, steep cliffs rise from the sea, providing nesting sites for huge colonies of seabirds, including Atlantic murres, black-legged kittiwakes, northern razorbills and one of the world's largest colonies of gannets (the second-largest in North America). Just off the shore is a unique, tower-like rock formation known as The Stack. This too is home to thousands of birds; the photo opportunities here are excellent. Also along the cape shore, near Witless Bay, is a seabird sanctuary made up of three offshore islands: Gull, Green and Great islands. Boat trips to the islands, where puffins, Atlantic razorbills, southern black kittiwakes, black-legged kittiwakes, great black-backed gulls and numerous other seabirds can be seen, are available.

The boardwalks at Point Pelee National Park in Ontario make birdwatching easy at this hotspot.

The Maritime Provinces

Canada's Maritime Provinces of New Brunswick, Nova Scotia and Prince Edward Island collectively offer beautiful scenery and excellent birding.

New Brunswick

Much of New Brunswick is dominated by coniferous and mixed forests interspersed with many lakes and rivers. There are large areas of freshwater marsh, especially along the St. John River, large expanses of peat bog and narrow salt marshes in many coastal areas on the Bay of Fundy. Topographically, the area ranges from barrier islands to mountains. As a result, it's not surprising that 40 percent of all the bird species ever recorded in North America have been seen in the province. The birding is surprisingly good on New Brunswick all year round. In April the summer residents start to arrive, including great blue herons, ruby-crowned kinglets, killdeers and warblers. Raptor flights are sometimes seen along the coast, and large numbers of waterbirds, particularly

Murres raise their young on the Newfoundland coast.

An arctic tern on Machias Seal Island, off the coast of New Brunswick.

ducks and geese, are on the move. In May the warblers and other songbirds arrive. The southbound migration of warblers, flycatchers and other birds gets under way in August, when immense concentrations of Bonaparte's gulls and phalaropes are also seen. In September the songbird migration continues and raptor flights are common; waterbirds such as loons, scoters and grebes concentrate in coastal locations in preparation for migration. Winter residents such as oldsquaws, roughlegged hawks, Iceland gulls, northern shrikes and snow buntings begin to arrive in October.

Grand Manan Island. Located in the Bay of Fundy between New Brunswick and Nova Scotia, Grand Manan Island is one of the best places in the entire northeast to see migrating songbirds and shorebirds; many rarities are spotted. In addition, the seabirds on the island and on nearby Seal Machias Island include petrels, guillemots, gulls, terns, shearwaters, jaegers, Atlantic puffins and Arctic terns.

Nova Scotia

Nova Scotia offers fascinating history and beautiful scenery along with superior birding. Boreal birds include spruce grouse, flycatchers, boreal chickadees, evening grosbeaks and many warblers. In addition, the Eastern Shore and Cape Breton regions offer cormorants, terns, eiders and guillemots, among other seabirds. The spectacular Cabot Trail in Cape Breton Highlands National Park shouldn't be missed. Acadia University operates a banding station at Brier Island at the end of Digby Neck in the Bay of Fundy. Heavy concentrations of shorebirds can be seen in the fall at the mudflats of the Minas Basin, and large numbers of shore and wading birds are found in the marshes of the Amherst Point Wildlife Sanctuary near the New Brunswick border every spring. In summer bald eagles and ospreys are frequently seen soaring along the coast; there are about 200 pairs of nesting bald eagles in Nova Scotia.

Prince Edward Island

A variety of habitats in easy proximity and a good road system make birding on Prince Edward Island a pleasure. The island is an important stopover point on the migration route. The piping plover, one of Canada's endangered species, nests on the beaches of PEI National Park. Ducks are plentiful on ponds and marshes throughout the island. The north shore is a good spot for observing northern gannets, scoters, oldsquaws and cormorants. Large numbers of warblers summer in the woods; the Townshend Woodlot on the Souris Line Road is a superb spot to appreciate warbler diversity. Bald eagles are scarce on Prince Edward Island, but many ospreys can be seen, especially in the area around Malpeque Bay.

The seabird sanctuary at Witless Bay, on the eastern coast of Newfoundland's Avalon Peninsula, is the home of this puffin.

Canadian Information Sources

Manitoba
Travel Manitoba
7155 Carlton Street
Winnipeg, Manitoba R3C 3H8
(204) 945-4066

New Brunswick
Peter Pearce
Canadian Wildlife Service
Box 400
Fredericton, New Brunswick   E3B 4Z9
(506) 452-3098

Tourism, Recreation and Heritage New
    Brunswick
Box 12345
Fredericton, New Brunswick   E3B 5C3
(800) 561-0123

New Brunswick Federation of Naturalists
New Brunswick Museum
277 Douglas Avenue
Saint John, New Brunswick   E2K 1E5
(506) 693-1196

Frank Longstaff, Naturalist
Shorecrest Lodge
North Head
Grand Manan, New Brunswick   E0G
    2M0
(506) 662-3216

Bill Daggett
New Brunswick Tourism
Anchorage Park, Seal Cove
Grand Manan, New Brunswick   E0G
    3B0
(506) 662-3215

Nova Scotia
Nova Scotia Bird Society
Nova Scotia Museum
1747 Summer Street
Halifax, Nova Scotia   B3H 3A6

Nova Scotia Department of Tourism and
    Culture
Box 456
Halifax, Nova Scotia   B3J 2R5
(902) 424-4247

Ontario
Ontario Ministry of Tourism and
    Recreation
77 Bloor Street West
Toronto, Ontario   M7A 2R9
(416) 965-8208

Federation of Ontario Naturalists
355 Lesmill Road
Don Mills, Ontario   M3B 2WB
(416) 444-8419

Prince Edward Island
Visitor Services
Box 940
Charlottetown, Prince Edward
    Island   C1A 7M5
(800) 565-9060

PEI Natural History Society
PEI Museum and Heritage Foundation
2 Kent Street
Charlottetown, Prince Edward
    Island   C1A 1M6
(902) 892-9127

Yukon
Yukon Tourism
Box 2703
Whitehorse, Yukon Territory   Y1A 2C6

Yukon Conservation Society
Box 4163
Whitehorse, Yukon Territory   Y1A 3T3

A gannet colony at Cape St. Mary's seabird sanctuary, on the Avalon Peninsula of Newfoundland.

Spectacular bird cliffs characterize the coasts of Newfoundland and Labrador.

CENTRAL AND SOUTH AMERICA
Mexico

The variety of birds in Mexico, so close to the United States, make it a prime birding destination. The terrain ranges from desert to tropical rain forest—an excellent place to gain experience in neotropical birdwatching.

Northeast Mexico. The Gulf of Mexico borders this region on the east, while inland the territory ranges from desert to rugged mountains to tropical forest. Numerous waterfowl and migrant shorebirds can be seen in the winter, and dry-country birds such as cactus wrens, sparrows and finches can be seen. In the southern part of the region tropical forests reach their northern limit; parrots are common, and ivory-billed woodcreepers, Amazon kingfishers, yellow-throated euphonias are also found.

Oaxaca. This old city in south-central Mexico is a good place for birding in general, and for seeing as many as twenty-six endemic Mexican species in particular. The variety of habitats is remarkable: arid desert, woodlands, riparian forest and cloud forest. The endemic birds that can be seen include dusky and bumblebee hummingbirds, golden vireos, bridled sparrows, pileated flycatchers and red-headed tanagers. An outstanding time to visit Oaxaca is at Christmas, when the birding is good and the colorful local holiday celebrations are in full swing.

Palenque and the Yucatán. The area around the ancient Mayan city of Palenque has more different kinds of birds than anywhere else in Mexico, in addition to fascinating Mayan ruins. Parrots, toucans, wrens, tanagers, flycatchers, doves, trogons, motmots, antbirds, hummingbirds, warblers and raptors are all easily seen—many birders notch up 200 birds on an average visit. The extensive Usumacinta marshes offer many wetlands species, including snail kites, double-striped thick-knees and pinnated bitterns. Many wintering birds from North America can be seen in the Yucatán. Resident birds include Yucatán jays, Yucatán wrens, orange orioles,

Despite its name, the Amazon kingfisher can be seen at its northern limit is northeastern Mexico.

The Usumacinta marshes in the Yucatan are the right habitat for pinnated bitterns.

cinnamon hummingbirds and cave swallows. The saltwater marshes on the coast are home to a large flock of greater flamingos, among other shorebirds.

Costa Rica

If there is one true birding paradise, it is Costa Rica. This small country (roughly the size of West Virginia) is home to nearly 800 species of all sorts. Divided down the middle by rugged mountain ranges, Costa Rica has many different habitats—from saltwater marshes to cloud forest, with many intermediate zones. Over thirty species of hummingbird, ten different trogons, and all sorts of woodcreepers, wrens and many other birds are easily seen. Late March and early April are particularly good times to visit.

The Central Plateau. Much of this region is cloud forest contained within national parks. Species that can be seen here include black-faced solitaires and wrenthrushes.

Cordillera Central. This rugged volcanic range reaches well over 10,000 feet (3,000 m) in places. The birds here include fiery-throated hummingbirds, yellow-thighed finches, tanagers, raptors and many others.

Pacific lowlands. Many lowland forest species are found here, including scarlet macaws, trogons, wrens, warblers, flycatchers and much more. Three-wattled bellbirds have been seen—and heard—in this area. Waterbirds, raptors and parrots are seen at the mouth of the Rio Tarcoles. The Carara Biological Preserve is one of the sanctuaries here.

Guanacaste region. A semi-arid region, Guanacaste is a good place to see many birds also seen further north in Mexico, including cinnamon hummingbirds. Santa Rosa National Park is an excellent birding locale for such birds as the double-striped thick-knee. Its beautiful sand beaches are also the breeding ground for the endangered Ridley's sea turtle.

Monteverde Cloud Forest Preserve. Straddling the Continental Divide in the Cordillera de Tilaran, this incredible preserve is the home of the resplendent quetzal. More than 300 other species are found here, including some amazing species of hummingbirds such as the magenta-throated woodstar.

San Isidro. The forests around this town are at a lower elevation and contain many sorts of hummingbirds, tanagers, flycatchers, honeycreepers and more—eighty species is an average tally.

La Selva Field Station. This research station has guest facilities and 1,400 acres (560 ha) of tropical rain forest. It is possible to see over 400 species, including toucans, flycatchers, tanagers, cotingas, and hummingbirds.

Two private companies offering tours of Costa Rica are:

Extraordinary Expeditions
Box 2793
Alameda, CA 94501
(415) 523-9263

Robert Sappenfield
Apartado 160
Turrialba, Costa Rica

Panama

Panama is the link between North and South America. As such, species from both continents are found here—some 900 in all, including the quetzal.

Eastern Panama. The birding sites in eastern Panama are numerous. Tocumen Marsh is excellent for raptors, hummingbirds, flycatchers and waterbirds. The famed Pipeline Road runs through lowland forest. Unbelievable numbers of woodcreepers, antbirds, flycatchers, finches, tanagers, honeycreepers, toucans and parrots can be seen here. Another famous birding path, the Achiote Road, provides a similar experience. Mudflats near Panama Viejo are an important place for waders and other waterbirds.

Western Panama. The high elevation of the western region takes a little getting used to, but the birding is worth it. The resplendent quetzal is seen on the Boquete Trail, as are emerald toucanets, black-capped flycatchers and many other birds. Other birds found in this part of the country include the amazing three-wattled bellbird, warblers, tanagers, trogons, parakeets and mountain robins.

Belize

Tiny Belize is only 170 by 60 miles (272 by 96 km), yet some 500 bird species have been recorded here. The average week-long trip could add over 200 birds to a life list. Keel-billed toucans, scarlet macaws, red-footed boobies, boat-billed herons and jabiru storks mingle with parrots, hummingbirds, trogons, woodcreepers, cotingas, tanagers, flycatchers and honeycreepers. The dry season in Belize is between February and May; the rains come between June and August. A good time for birders is between October and February.

The Navira Swamp on Trinidad's east coast is the home of black-crested antshrikes.

The orange-billed nightingale-thrush can be seen in the Aripo range of Trinidad.

Trinidad and Tobago

Just 10 miles (16 km) off the coast of Venezuela, the island of Trinidad offers an incredible birding experience. Several famous sites and preserves make it easy to see many of over 400 species that inhabit the island—an average trip will probably yield about 150 to 200 birds. For those whose interest in flying creatures extends beyond birds, Trinidad also has 600 butterfly species. The neighboring island of Tobago also has many birds, but most visitors prefer to relax on its beautiful beaches after the excitement of birding on Trinidad. Interestingly, the greater bird of paradise can be found in its wild state on Tobago. In 1909, when the bird was in danger of extinction on New Guinea, some were imported to Tobago, where they thrived in the similar climate.

Nariva Swamp and Arena Forest. Birds found in the Arena Forest include colonies of yellow-rumped caciques and tanagers, woodpeckers and trogons are common. In the huge Nariva Swamp on the east coast, birds to be seen include black-crested antshrikes, silvered ant-birds, green-throated mangos, green kingfishers, limpkins, black-shouldered kites and many other marsh birds. Hundreds of red-bellied macaws roost in the palm trees every evening.

Aripo Range. This rugged range is the home of the yellow-legged thrush (found only above 2,000 feet [600 m]), the orange-billed nightingale-thrush and the blue-capped tanager.

Northern Range and Asa Wright Nature Center. The birding here can be fast and furious, with motmots, bearded bellbirds, chestnut woodpeckers, bat falcons, oilbirds and keel-billed toucans among the possibilities. One of the best-known hot spots in South America, the Asa Wright Nature Center is a highlight of any tour to Trinidad.

Caroni Swamp. Shorebirds and marsh birds are more abundant here than anywhere else on the island. The spectacular evening flight of the scarlet ibis occurs here. Other birds to be seen include red-capped cardinals, gray-necked wood-rails, strong-billed woodcreepers and other birds of the mangroves.

Bearded bellbirds are among the amazing species found at the famed Asa Wright Nature Center on Trinidad.

The colorful keel-billed toucan is one of the many remarkable birds found in Belize.

The forests of Costa Rica are home to several species of tanager, including this blue-capped tanager.

The aptly named resplendent quetzal can be seen at the Monteverde Cloud Forest Preserve in Costa Rica.

Venezuela

Nearly 1,300 species can be spotted in Venezuela amid a variety of habitats ranging from coastal desert to cloud forest. It's a good place to get started in tropical birding.

Henri Pittier National Park. This giant preserve has several habitats ranging from arid scrub to cloud forest. The range of birds is astonishing: white-tipped quetzals, groove-billed toucanets, blue-capped tanagers, blood-eared parakeets, buffy hummingbirds, pearly-vented tody tyrants, black-backed antshrikes and many more.

The llanos. The vast savannahs of Venezuela are known as *llanos*. Birds are abundant here, and also easy to see. Among them are seven species of ibis and numerous herons, sunbitterns, hoatzins, thornbirds, scarlet macaws and raptors.

The Andes. Many intriguing birds are found in the Andes, including bearded helmet-crests, Andean tit-spinetails, ochre-browed thistletails, crested and golden-headed quetzals, many flycatchers and tanagers, and many others.

The pearly-vented tody tyrant is found in Henry Pittier National Park in Venezuela.

Scarlet ibises take to the air in Trinidad. These vivid birds are the only members of the ibis family to be so brightly colored.

Peru

The unusual geography of Peru acounts for its incredible bird life—nearly 1,700 species. The cold waters along the coast support some of the largest seabird colonies on earth, but there one of the world's driest deserts meets the ocean. The second-highest mountain in the western hemisphere is in Peru; at the foot of the eastern slope of the Andes lies a vast expanse of Amazonian rain forest. New species are still being found in Peru.

Amazonia. The tropical birds to be seen along this mighty river include many woodcreepers, flycatchers, kingfishers, ovenbirds, parrots, toucans, antbirds and raptors. In addition, many endemic species are seen, including the spectacular black-necked red cotinga.

Andes. The astonishing Andean cock-of-the-rock is the bird to see here, along with such high-altitude birds as Andean geese and bright-rumped yellow finches.

Paracas Peninsula. The ocean and the desert meet at this national nature preserve. Boobies, pelicans, gulls, cormorants, terns, skimmers and many migrant shorebirds can be seen.

Ecuador and the Galápagos Islands

A birding trip to Ecuador is often combined with an excursion to the Galápagos Islands, owned by Ecuador. Although Ecuador is quite small, some 1,400 species have been recorded there, including many endemics. In the Andes region near Quito the colorful toucan barbet can be seen, as can many tanagers and amazing numbers and sorts of hummingbirds. Many spectacular large birds can be seen in the cloud forests on the western side of the Andes, while many of the endemic species are found in the scrub and woodlands of the coastal regions.

The Galápagos Islands are in the Pacific Ocean 600 miles (960 km) off the coast of Ecuador. The thirteen main islands and several smaller islands are all now an Ecuadorian national park. It is here that Charles Darwin, observing the many highly specialized types of finch in 1835, began to formulate his theory of natural selection. The birds of the Galápagos are truly remarkable examples of isolated evolution: frigate birds, blue-footed, red-footed and masked boobies, pelicans, flamingos, lava gulls, herons, flycatchers, oystercatchers, swallow-tail gulls, Galápagos doves, Galápagos hawks, red-billed tropic birds, flightless cormorants, shearwaters, Galápagos storm petrels, owls, hawks—and even penguins.

The climate of the Galápagos is surprisingly cool because of the nearby Humboldt and Peruvian ocean currents, which originate in the Antarctic. From December through March the temperatures are in the 80s and 90s (high 20s and low 30s C); the temperature begins to drop in April. The strongest trade winds and lowest temperatures (60s and 70s [high teens and low 20s C]) are found in late September.

Tours of the Galápagos are offered by:

Inca Floats
1311 North 63 Street
Emeryville, CA 94608
(415) 420-1550

Despite the high altitude, Andean geese thrive in Peru's Andes Mountains.

Jervis Island in the Galapagos is the home of this pelican.

Flamingos are found on Floreana in the Galapagos.

This red-footed booby was photographed on Tower Island in the Galapagos.

The blue-footed booby shown here was photographed on Isabela Island in the Galapagos. The photographer was Dr. Bill Hardy for Holbrook Travel.

Gull on Tower Island in the Galapagos.

One of the more unusual of the many strange birds on the Galapagos is the flightless cormorant.

Argentina

The eighth-largest country in the world offers some excellent regions for birding.

The Pampas. These vast plains support a huge number of birds, including snail kites, black-headed ducks, greater rheas, swans and numerous waterfowl.

Patagonia. Distant and bleak, this area nonetheless offers good birding, especially at the Valdez Peninsula and Punta Tombo. A million-strong colony of Magellanic penguins is found at Punta Tombo. The desert scrub of the Valdez Peninsula is home for Darwin's rheas and many intriguing small birds. At Tierra del Fuego National Park at the southern tip of Patagonia, condors are common, and flightless steamer ducks, austral blackbirds and a surprising number of other birds can be seen.

Los Glaciares National Park. In the steppe-like country here two unusual and rare birds are among those found: Magellanic plovers and hooded grebes.

Finca El Rey National Park. Birds of the tropical rain forest at the base of the Andes can be seen here, including the rare rufous-throated dipper. The preserve at Pozuelos Lake is a good place to see waterbirds, including flamingos.

Brazil

Brazil is the largest country in South America, and the fifth largest in the world. Within this vast territory of well over 3 million square miles (7.8 million km) is found an amazing array of habitats and birds. Although the Amazon Basin covers much of the land, there are also extensive plains areas and spectacular mountains covered with cloud forest.

The Amazon. Endemic birds such as the opal-crowned manakin abound in the forests along the Amazon. Development is cutting down the forests, but the million acres of Amazonia National Park still harbor the golden parakeet, a number of different antbirds, cotingas and eagles, as well as many others.

Cerrado region. Central Brazil con-

Many waterbirds are seen in the *pantanal*. Here wood storks congregate in a tree.

tains expansive *cerrados*, or grasslands, that are home to toco toucans, redwinged tinamous, rheas, flycatchers and more. Brasilia National Park preserves the grasslands in their wild state; much of this territory is now agricultural.

Pantanal region. Extensive marshland, or *pantanal*, is found in southwestern Brazil. These wetlands are covered with incredible numbers of waterbirds, including jabiru and giant storks. The hyacinth macaw is also seen here.

Itatiaia National Park. Many spectacular birds are seen in southeastern Brazil, including hummingbirds, tanagers, antbirds and cotingas.

The marshland region of southwestern Brazil is known as the *pantanal*. The giant stork can be seen.

Scarlet ibises feed in the marshy Brazilian *pantanal*.

Antarctica

The Antarctic Peninsula, the Falkland Islands, the South Georgia Islands and the smaller islands that fringe the peninsula are as remote as it is possible for a birder to get. These distant, cold, windswept places are hard and expensive to reach, but for the dedicated birdwatcher (especially penguin lovers) they are definitely worthwhile.

South Georgia Islands. Huge rookeries of king penguins are found here; in contrast is the endemic tiny South Georgia pipit.

Falkland Islands. Penguins—Magellanic, rockhopper, macaroni, king, gentoo, Adelie and chinstrap—and albatrosses are found here.

Antarctic Peninsula. Adelie, gentoo and chinstrap penguins abound; albatrosses with 11-foot (3 m) wingspreads can also be seen.

Penguins are found only in the southern hemisphere. This colony was photographed by Victoria Underwood for Society Expeditions.

Central and South America Tourist Boards and Embassies

Argentina
Argentine Embassy
1600 New Hampshire Avenue, NE
Washington, DC 20017
(202) 939-6400

Argentine Tourist Office
1270 Avenue of the Americas
New York, NY 10020
(212) 581-1018

Belize
Embassy of Belize
1576 Eye Street, NW
Washington, DC 20006
(202) 289-1416

Brazil
Brazilian Embassy
Washington, DC 20015
(202) 745-2700

Consulate General of Brazil
630 Fifth Avenue
New York, NY 10111
(212) 757-3080

Brazilian Tourism Bureau
150 West 47 Street
New York, NY 10036
(212) 575-9406

Costa Rica
Embassy of Costa Rica
1825 Connecticut Avenue, NW
Washington, DC 20008
(202) 234-2945

Consulate General of Costa Rica
80 Wall Street
New York, NY 10005
(212) 425-2620

Tourist Board of Costa Rica
630 Fifth Avenue
New York, NY 10111
(212) 245-6370

Ecuador
Embassy of Ecuador
2535 15 Street, NW
Washington, DC 20011
(202) 234-7200

Mexico
Embassy of Mexico
2829 16 Street, NW
Washington, DC 20011
(202) 234-6000

Consulate General of Mexico
8 East 41 Street
New York, NY 10017
(212) 689-0456

Mexican National Tourist Council
405 Park Avenue
New York, NY 10022
(212) 755-7261

Panama
Panama Embassy
2862 McGill Terrace, NW
Washington, DC 20008
(202) 483-1407

Consulate General of Panama
1270 Avenue of the Americas
New York, NY 10020
(212) 246-3771

Panama Government Tourist Bureau
309 East 49 Street
New York, NY 10017
(212) 826-9039

Peru
Embassy of Peru
1700 Massachusetts Avenue, NW
Washington, DC 20008
(202) 833-9860

Consulate General of Peru
805 Third Avenue
New York, NY 10022
(212) 644-2850

Trinidad and Tobago
Embassy of Trinidad and Tobago
1708 Massachusetts Avenue, NW
Washington, DC 20008
(202) 467-6490

Trinidad and Tobago Tourist Board
400 Madison Avenue, Suite 712
New York, NY 10017
(212) 838-7750

Trinidad and Tobago Tourist Board
200 S.E. First Street, Suite 702
Miami, FL 33131
(305) 374-2056

Venezuela
Embassy of Venezuela
Information Service
2437 California Street, NW
Washington, DC 20008
(202) 797-3800

Venezuela Government Tourist Bureau
7 East 51 Street
New York, NY 10022
(212) 355-1101

This king penguin colony was photographed as part of a Project Antarctica trip by Society Expeditions.

Herons roost in a tree in the *pantanal* region of Brazil.

On St. Martin in the French West Indies, falconer Jean-Pierre Bordes raises his arm to receive a landing eagle.

THE CARIBBEAN ISLANDS

The many small islands scattered throughout the Caribbean are usually thought of simply as winter beach resorts, but from a birder's point of view they offer other rewards. Many islands have unusual endemic birds in addition to many fascinating winter migrants—Jamaica alone has twenty-six endemics. All the islands offer relaxed birdwatching that is never very far from a pleasant beach. The breeding season generally starts around the beginning of May, making this a good time to visit.

Dominican Republic
The Dominican Republic occupies two-thirds of the island of Hispaniola; the rest of the island is the country of Haiti. The Dominican Republic boasts delightful beaches and Santo Domingo, the oldest city in the Western Hemisphere. Over twenty endemic species of birds are found here, including the Hispaniolan woodpecker, Hispaniolan trogon and Hispaniolan lizard cuckoo, as well as many species found nowhere else in the Caribbean. Numerous shorebirds, waterbirds, cuckoos and warblers are residents and visitors.

The Lesser Antilles
This island group consists of the Windward and Leeward Islands, including Dominica, Grenada, Guadalupe, Martinique, Saba, St. Eustatius, St. Lucia, St. Martin and St. Vincent. Many endemic birds are found on the islands due to their evolutionary isolation from South America. Many rare parrots can be seen; other colorful birds, including many egrets, pelicans, warblers, humingbirds, sparrows and thrushes, are also present. Sugarbirds (a type of small yellow-breasted finch) are common, and frigate birds with 6-foot (2-m) wingspans can often be seen soaring offshore. Antillean crested hummingbirds, bananaquits and smooth-billed anis are all found here.

Jamaica
The rugged interior of Jamaica contrasts with the fringe of sandy beaches and coral reefs around the island. Many coastal mangrove swamps and salt marshes provide a home to herons, egrets and numerous migrant wading birds. Golden swallows, blue mountain vireos and white-eyed thrushes are among the birds found in the mountains.

Caribbean Information

Dominican Republic
Embassy of the Dominican Republic
1715 22 Avenue, NW
Washington, DC   20008
(202) 332-6280

Dominican Republic Consulate
17 West 60 Street
New York, NY   10023
(212) 265-0630

Jamaica
Jamaica Tourist Board
2 Dag Hammarskjold Plaza
New York, NY   10017
(212) 688-7650

Lesser Antilles
French West Indies Tourist Board
628 Fifth Avenue
New York, NY   10020
(212) 757-1125

Grenada Tourist Information
141 East 44 Street
New York, NY   10017
(212) 686-9554

St. Lucia Tourist Board
41 East 42 Street
New York, NY   10017
(212) 867-2950

St. Maarten-Saba-St. Eustatius Tourist
Office
275 Seventh Avenue
New York, NY   10001
(212) 989-0000

Caribbean Tours
Wonder Bird Tours
500 Fifth Avenue
New York, NY   10110
(212) 840-5961

Egrets are often seen in the Lesser Antilles, where they are called cowbirds because of the way they hitch rides on passing cows.

EUROPE AND THE NEAR EAST

Austria

Although the Alps cover two-thirds of Austria, and although it is a fairly small country, it has an unusual variety of bird life and a number of interesting places to see it. In the western alpine regions rock ptarmigans, hoopoes, alpine wall creepers and rock buntings can all be seen, as can many other alpine birds. A group of fifty to eighty vultures summers in the Hohe Tauern mountains near Salzburg. Only 30 miles (48 km) east of Vienna, heading toward the Hungarian border, the reed-bordered lakes of the Seewinkel region and the Neusiedler See offer many migrating shorebirds and northern European species, including herons, red-crested pochards, ferruginous ducks, sandpipers, stints, warblers, hoopoes, and the rare penduline tit. The nearby Neusiedl am See Lake Museum has excellent exhibits about the bird life in the region. Some 18 miles (29 km) southeast of Lake Neusiedl is the Andau preserve, which protects a number of European great bustards. At up to 45 pounds (20 kg), these are the heaviest birds that can fly; many other raptors can also be seen here. White storks nest on the roofs near here, and black storks are sometimes seen. The Furtner Teich reserve in Styria is only 32 acres (13 ha) of ponds and reed belts, but 235 species of birds have been seen there. It is also one of the oldest observation stations in the world; migration records have been kept since 1845. The Alpine Zoo at Innsbruck is a specialized zoo devoted to the fauna of the Alps. Specimens on exhibit include birds such as the hermit ibis and the bearded vulture, which have become extinct in their native habitat. Interestingly, excellent birding is found on the grounds of the Schoenbrunn Palace in Vienna—gray-headed woodpeckers, hawfinches and blue and great tits are all visible.

A heron stalks its prey on Lake Neusiedl near Vienna.

A heron and chicks on Lake Neusiedl.

Belgium

At Knokke-Heist on the Belgian coast, not far from Bruges, is the Zwin nature reserve. In the spring a number of breeding birds can be seen at this 300-acre (120-ha) salt marsh, including shelducks, oyster-catchers, avocets, lapwings, gulls, plovers and numerous wading birds. White storks, graylag geese, golden orioles, crested larks and various warblers can also be seen. In addition, more than 500 birds of 100 different species can be seen in the large aviaries and ponds of the reserve.

Cyprus

Migrating birds crossing the eastern Mediterranean from Africa to Europe frequently stop on Cyprus. Some 375 different species have been recorded. Common birds on Cyprus include the red-rumped swallow, black-headed wagtail, reed warbler, Cyprus warbler, griffon vulture, Kentish plover and little grebe. The unspoiled Toodos mountain region is good for birdwatching. For more information on birding in Cyprus, contact:

Cyprus Ornithological Society
4 Kanaris Street
Strovolos 154
Nicosia, Cyprus

Denmark

The best birding in Denmark is found in north Jutland and on the island of Bornholm. North Jutland is pounded by the North Sea on the west and the Baltic Sea on the east; the heaths, dunes and bogs make it a strategically placed resting point for migrating birds. Skagen, on the northern tip of the peninsula, is a good location for large numbers of migrating birds in the spring and fall. Those interested in raptors will find the eagle sanctuary at Tuen, south of Skagen, fascinating. Golden and white-tailed eagles are featured; other eagles and falcons can also be seen. One of the largest bird sanctuaries in northern Europe is found at Ulvedbyt. This diked-in, marshy arm of the Lim Fjord shelters large numbers of breeding wading and diving birds, but is closed to the public. The birds can be seen well from the dike, however. The penguin house at the Aalborg Zoo is also worth a visit.

The Danish island of Bornholm in the Baltic Sea is an excellent spot to view migrating birds such as eagles, cranes, hawks and many smaller birds. In fact, Bornholm is sometimes called "The Island of Nightingales." It has a mild climate, abundant flora and beautiful white sand beaches. It is reached by a seven-hour ferry ride from Copenhagen.

For more information about birding in Denmark, contact:

Dansk Ornitologisk Forening
Vesterbrogade 140
1620 Kobenhavn V
Denmark

Storks nest on a platform in the Zwin nature preserve.

Faroe Islands

Rising out of the stormy Atlantic halfway between Norway and Iceland, the eighteen Faroe Islands are incredible havens for seabirds. The steep mountainsides provide breeding grounds for colonies of gannets, puffins, guillemots and many others. The island of Mykines, where vast numbers of birds breed undisturbed, is considered the highlight of any birding trip to the Faroes. In summer, the island is reached by boat or by helicopter. There are very few inhabitants on Mykines, so any visit must be a day trip. During June and July, the best time to visit the Faroes, the local tourist association arranges trips to Mykines and other islands.

The Faroe Islands can be reached by air or ferry from Denmark; the ferry ride takes about thirty-six hours. This is not the place for those seeking a luxurious vacation. The Faroes are windy and *cold*—at the peak of summer on a sunny day the temperature might reach 60°F (16°C)—so bring warm, windproof clothing and waterproof boots.

France

The marshy region of the Rhône delta on the Mediterranean coast of France near Arles (about 50 miles [80 km] from Marseilles) is known as the Camargue. The area supports a very large and famous colony of greater flamingos. Numerous resident and migrant birds are found here, including red-crested pochards, plovers, bitterns and collared pratincoles. Many fascinating birds, including little bustards and calandra larks, are found in nearby areas. In the craggy Pyrenees mountains separating France from Spain numerous mountain species can be seen: golden eagles, Alpine choughs, ring ouzels and the rare lammergeier.

Great Britain (England, Scotland and Wales)

A birding trip to Great Britain in late spring can add some 200 birds to a life list. The marshy fen country of Norfolk, north of London, has extensive reed beds and lagoons, providing the right habitat for bitterns, avocets, spoonbills, nightingales and other birds. Two important bird sanctuaries are run here by the Norfolk Naturalist's Trust and the Royal Society for the Protection of Birds. Elsewhere in England whinchats, stonechats, warblers, linnets, cuckoos, wagtails, curlews, skylarks and many other species are found. The steep cliffs of the Farne Islands, in the North Sea just below the border with Scotland, have been a bird sanctuary for centuries. Large colonies of fulmars, puffins, razorbills, kittiwakes, gulls and terns breed here.

In Scotland, the Cairngorms region offers a great variety of interesting birds, including capercaillies, Scottish crossbills, black grouse and snow buntings. The Western Isles (Outer Hebrides) include the islands of Skye, North Uist, South Uist and Lewis. Birds to be seen here include golden eagles, red-necked phalaropes, graylag geese, short-eared owls and golden plovers. Numerous pelagic birds, including Manx shearwaters, petrels and Arctic skuas are found.

Snowdonia National Park in Wales can provide glimpses of peregrine falcons, ring ouzels, willow ptarmigans, red grouse and red kites.

Two private companies offering personalized bird tours are:

Richard Crossley
Abbots Hood
Halberton, Devon
England

Steve Gantlett
18 Old Woman's Lane
Cley-Next-the-Sea
Holt, Norfolk
England NR25 7TY

Snow buntings are found in the Cairngorms region of Scotland.

Birding Scotland

Scotland is a favorite European birding spot, combining good birding with stunning scenery. Organized and private birding tours originating in Scotland can be arranged through these addresses:

Mr. Michael Wigan
Borrobol Birding
Kinbrace
Sutherland
Scotland   KW11 6UB

US agent for Borrobol Birding:
Josephine Barr
519 Park Avenue
Kenilworth, IL 60043
(800) 323-5463/(312) 251-4110

Caledonian Wildlife
30 Culduthel Road
Inverness
Scotland   IV2 4AP

The marshes of the Camargue support a well-known colony of greater flamingos. Here one descends to a landing.

The area around Sutherland in Scotland, not far from the Borrobol Lodge.

Unusual waterbirds are seen at the Wildfowl Trust preserve in Slimbridge, England.

These ducks are at the Wildfowl Trust preserve in England.

Northern gannets breed on the cliffs of the Faroe Islands.

Greece

The variety of habitats in southern Greece make it a good place to spot most of the common Mediterranean species, such as spotted flycatchers and many kinds of warbler (especially during the spring migration). The best reason to go to Greece, however, is to bird on the island of Rhodes in the spring. Birds migrating north from Africa find Rhodes a handy landfall, and the nearby Turkish coast adds some additional variety. The island is famous for blue-cheeked bee-eaters; Eleanora's, red-footed and peregrine falcons can also be seen. Like Rhodes, the island of Crete is rich in birds migrating from Africa. Warblers and wrens abound, as do raptors such as golden eagles, lammergeiers and Eleanora's falcon.

Iceland

The spectacular scenery and unique geological features of Iceland are almost more interesting than the bird life. The island's steep cliffs and the abundant waters that surround it make it a paradise for seabirds of many sorts, including puffins. Birdwatching everywhere on Iceland is rewarding, but perhaps the one spot not to be missed is Lake Myvatn in the northeast. Among the birds that can be seen here are three species of duck found nowhere else in Europe: Barrow's goldeneye, harlequin and great northern diver. Also abundant in the area are red-necked phalaropes, blacktail godwits and snow buntings, among others. The coastal region of the northeastern Snaefalles peninsula, which includes the magnificent Breidtha fjord,

also has massive numbers of fulmars, wigeons, puffins, purple sandpipers, whooper swans, and the largest colony of arctic terns in Iceland. The beautiful Svalthufa bird cliffs are here.

On the south coast of Iceland near Selfoss, skuas nest on the sand plains. Near the village of Vik is a large and easily accessible colony of puffins; black-tailed godwits can also be seen. The incredible Westman Islands off the southern coast are largely uninhabited by anything except huge colonies of gannets, kittiwakes, fulmars, shearwaters and alcids of virtually every sort.

Because the Gulf Stream encircles and warms the island, Iceland is not as cold as its name suggests. The best time for a birding visit is in the late spring or summer, when the temperature is in the

A common sight near Lake Myvatn in Iceland is black-tailed godwits.

Natty harlequin ducks take to the water in Iceland.

50s and 60s (low teens C). The weather in Iceland changes rapidly, however, so bring water- and windproof outerwear and sturdy shoes.

Ireland

Ireland is the first landfall in winter for many birds that breed in the arctic regions. Notable species include pale-bellied brants and barnacle geese, whooper swans, golden plovers and black-tailed godwits. Also present are the rare Bewick's swan and Greenland white-fronted goose. Relatively few birds are resident in Ireland, so the fall migration in September and October and the spring migration in April and May are the best times to visit. Coastal headlands and off-shore islands are the best sites.

Cape Clear Bird Observatory in County Cork is famous as a site to see large seabirds in the fall, particularly skuas and shearwaters. Many rare migrants and vagrants can also be seen. Extensive bird-banding operations are carried out at the Copeland Bird Observatory in County Down. Gull, tern and Manx shearwater colonies can be seen, as can breeding eiders. Ireland also has more than sixty bird sanctuaries. One of the most accessible is the Wexford Wildfowl Reserve on the grassy fields of North Slob. In the winter the reserve attracts vast numbers of geese, swans, ducks and wading species, as well as other waterbirds and birds of prey.

For more information about birding in Ireland, contact:

Irish Wildbird Conservancy
Rutledge House, 8 Longford Place
Monkstown, County Dublin
Ireland

Israel

At the crossroads of three continents, Israel has a wide range of habitats and climates in a small area. The varied terrain attracts over 400 species of birds, which can be seen in the many nature preserves across the country. The city of Eilat, at the northern tip of the Red Sea, is situated in the Syrian-African Rift Valley—one of the principal migration routes for birds traveling from Africa to Europe from February to May. Millions of birds—raptors, storks, pelicans and many others—take advantage of the warm air currents that rise above the steep cliffs of the valley, making Eilat a world-class place to observe bird migration. More than 150 migrating species can easily be seen. Resident species such as the bulbul, little green bee-eater, wheatear and Barbary falcon can be seen as well. The Bird Watching Centre in Eilat offers guided tours three times a week; there is also a self-guiding trail.

For more information about birding in Israel, contact:

Bird Watching Centre
King Solomon Hotel
Box 774
Eilat Israel

Society for the Protection of
Nature in Israel
4 Hashfela Street
Tel Aviv 66183 Israel

Mallorca

The Mediterranean island of Mallorca, south of Barcelona, is famed for the variety of birds that can be seen during the spring migration, especially from mid- to late April. The chances of seeing an unusual bird are excellent. Prime sites for birdwatching are mostly in the northeast of the island. The Albufera marsh, the largest on Mallorca, is now a reserve where purple herons, garganeya and moustached warblers can be seen. In the mountains are crossbills, booted eagles, firecrests and black vultures. Cape Salinas in the south provides views of shearwaters and other seabirds, including the extremely rare Andouin's gull. The nearby salt marshes teem with wading birds; when weather conditions are right, this is an excellent place to spot rarities.

Norway

The largest bird sanctuaries in Europe are found in Norway among the Lofoten islands beyond the Arctic Circle. Although these spectacular islands are hard to reach, the trip is worthwhile. From the end of May to the middle of July, when the midnight sun never dips below the horizon, millions of seabirds can be seen, including curlews, guillemots, puffins, fulmars, kittywakes and cormorants. The island of Røst, about 60 miles (96 km) from the mainland, is a good starting point. The largest bird sanctuaries are found on the nearby islands of Vedøy and Storfjell, both inhabited solely by birds. Visiting the Lofoten islands is something of an expedition: the quickest route is to fly from Oslo to Bodø or Narvik (about two to three hours), and then on by boat (about six hours) to the islands. For more information about accommodations and transportation, contact:

Nordland Travel Association
Postboks 434
8001 Bodø
Norway

Somewhat more accessible than the Lofoten islands are the bird rocks of Runde, in the fjord country about 16 miles (26 km) from Ålesund (about an hour's flight from Oslo). The mountainous island of Runde is only a few square miles in area, but the steep precipices, some over 1,000 feet (300 m) high, are home to over two million breeding sea birds and comprise the second largest bird sanctuary in Norway. Puffins are seen in vast numbers, as are kittiwakes, razorbills, oystercatchers, gannets, fulmars, gulls, guillemots and more. Because breeding birds are strictly protected by law, the best time to visit is in the summer, starting in early July. There are no hotels on the island, so visitors must arrive and depart by boat from Alesund; the trip takes about two hours each way. For more information, contact:

Ålesund Tourist Office
Rasmus Rønnebergsgate 15b
Postboks 537
Ålesund N-6001
Norway

Coto Donana, Spain's famous bird reserve, is a good place to spot purple gallinules.

The famed bird rocks of Norway are home to huge colonies of black-legged kittiwakes and other sea birds.

Spain

A birding trip to Spain could add some 200 species to a life list. Near Seville is one of the most famous reserves in the world, the Coto Doñana. Marbled teals, purple gallinules and great spotted cuckoos are among the rarities that can be seen. The wetlands of the Marismas delta of the Guadalquivir River are rich in waterbirds and raptors, including imperial eagles, crested coots, black-winged stilts and avocets. The valleys of the Tagus region are full of raptors: red kites, great bustards and Montagu's harriers are all commonly seen. The lakes of the Mancha plateau surrounding Madrid provide a variety of habitats for waterfowl. Over twenty species of wading bird can be observed, as well as grebes, terns and warblers. In the mountainous Pyrenees region of northeastern Spain many raptors, including griffons, kites, Egyptian vultures and even lammergeiers, can be seen. The alpine regions of the range offer alpine accentors, snowfinches, alpine wallcreepers, white-backed woodpeckers, booted eagles and black wheatears, to name just a few. The Ebro delta region on the Mediterranean coast is an excellent area for waterbirds. Egrets, waders, terns and waterfowl of all sorts can be seen, including purple herons, little bitterns and slender-billed gulls.

Mr. Spain

Tom Gullick is known as birding's Mister Spain—a misnomer, since he also leads bird tours in Morocco. After years of living and birdwatching in Spain, Mr. Gullick has access to many productive private areas not seen by the general public. His private tours by Range Rover are legendary. For more information write:

Mrs. Monique Parker
5 Tile Barn Close
Farnborough, Hants.
England   GU14 8LS

Turkey

At the crossroads of Europe and Asia, the varied terrain of Turkey in the spring offers the whole spectrum of Eurasian species and then some. The Manyas Golu reserve along the Sea of Marmara is home to the very rare Dalmatian pelican, many wading birds and nesting herons. In the Aladag Mountains golden orioles, Nubian shrikes, crimson-winged finches, Caspian snowcocks and ring ouzels are just some of the birds that can be seen. The scrublands along the Euphrates river offer Dead Sea sparrows, blue-cheeked bee-eaters, eagle owls and more.

Tourist Offices

Excellent—and free—sources of up-to-date information about overseas travel are tourist offices operated by national governments. When contacting a tourist office, be sure to mention your interest in birding (or any other special activity)—a surprising amount of detailed information that is very helpful when planning a trip may be available. Embassies and consulates also often have tourist information and details about customs regulations, health precautions and so on.

Austria

Austrian Consulate General
31 East 69 Street
New York, NY   10021
(212) 737-6400

Austrian Embassy
2343 Massachusetts Avenue, NW
Washington, DC   20008
(202) 483-4474

Austrian National Tourist Office
500 Fifth Avenue
New York, NY 10110
212 944 6880

Belgium

Belgian Embassy
3330 Garfield Street, NW
Washington, DC   20008
(202) 333-6900

Belgian Consulate General
50 Rockefeller Plaza
New York, NY   10020
(212) 586-5110

Belgian Tourist Office
745 Fifth Avenue
New York, NY   10151
(212) 758-8130

Cyprus

Embassy of Cyprus
2211 R Street, NW
Washington, DC 20007
(202) 462-5772

Cyprus Tourism Organization
13 East 40 Street
New York, NY 10016
(212) 868-6016

Denmark (including Iceland, Greenland, Faroe Islands)

Danish Embassy
3200 Whitehaven Road, NW
Washington, DC 20008
(202) 234-4300

Danish Tourist Board
655 Third Avenue
New York NY 10017
(212) 949-2333

Danish Tourist Board
8929 Wilshire Boulevard
Los Angeles, CA 90211
(213) 854-1549

Danish Tourist Board
150 North Michigan Avenue
Chicago, IL 60601
(312) 726-1120

France

Embassy of France
2221 Kalorama Road
Washington, DC 20008
(202) 387-2666

French Government Tourist Office
628 Fifth Avenue
New York, NY 10020
(212) 757-1125

Consulate General of France
934 Fifth Avenue
New York, NY 10021
(212) 606-3600

Great Britain (England, Scotland, Wales)

British Embassy
3100 Massachusetts Avenue, NW
Washington, DC 20008
(202) 462-1340

British Tourist Authority
40 West 57 Street
New York, NY 10019
(212) 581-4700

Greece

Embassy of Greece
2211 Massachusetts Avenue, NW
Washington, DC 20008
(202) 332-2727

Greek Consulate General
69 East 79 Street
New York, NY 10021
(212) 988-5500

Greek National Tourist Organization
645 Fifth Avenue
New York, NY 10022
(212) 421-5777

Ireland

Embassy of Ireland
2234 Massachusetts Avenue, NW
Washington, DC 20008
(202) 462-3939

Irish Tourist Board
757 Third Avenue
New York, NY 10017
(212) 418-0800

Israel

Embassy of Israel
3514 International Drive, NW
Washington, DC 20008
(202) 364-5400

Consulate General of Israel
800 Second Avenue
New York, NY 10017
(212) 697-5500

Israel Government Tourist Office
350 Fifth Avenue
New York, NY 10118
(800) 367-4668/(212) 691-2361

Israel Government Tourist Office
6380 Wilshire Boulevard
Los Angeles, CA 90048
(213) 658-7462

Israel Government Tourist Office
5 South Wabash Avenue
Chicago, IL 60603
(312) 782-4306

Norway

Embassy of Norway
2720 34 Street, NW
Washington, DC 20008
(202) 333-6000

Norwegian Tourist Board
655 Third Avenue
New York, NY 10017
(212) 949-2333

Spain (including Mallorca)

Embassy of Spain
2700 15 Street, NW
Washington, DC 20008
(202) 265-0190

Consulate General of Spain
150 East 58 Street
New York, NY 10022
(212) 355-4080

Spanish National Tourist Office
665 Fifth Avenue
New York, NY 10022
(212) 759-8822

Turkey

Embassy of Turkey
2523 Massachusetts Avenue, NW
Washington, DC 20008
(202) 483-5366

Turkish Government Tourism and
   Information Office
821 UN Plaza
New York, NY 10017
(212) 687-2194

AFRICA
Planning for Africa

A trip to Africa, especially eastern Africa, is every bird lover's fondest dream—in Kenya it is possible to see over 600 bird species in a startling range of habitats. An African trip, however, is a bit more complicated—and a lot more expensive—than some other trips, so advance knowledge and planning are crucial.

The simplest way to organize an excursion to Africa is through one of the tour operators specializing in wildlife or bird tours. It is possible to arrange air tickets, tour guides, lodgings and so on privately, but this has many pitfalls. To suggest just a few: considerably higher costs, currency exchange fees and other snarls, delayed (or no) refunds in case of cancellation, language barriers. If, despite this, you wish to proceed, contact the tourist offices of the countries you wish to visit. They can often provide a list of resident guides and tour operators in the country. Don't try the trip without hiring a knowledgeable guide— you won't see many birds.

Contact the embassies or consulates of the countries you plan to visit to get information about visas, customs, health precautions, currency restrictions, climate information and the like. Do this well in advance of the trip. Some medications should be started before departure, and customs clearances, visas and so on can take a while.

Serious birders travel with a vast array of binoculars, cameras and other optical gear. It is extremely important to bring all receipts and customs clearances with you. Bring along twice as much film as you think you will need and at least one spare battery for everything that requires one. Store all film in a refrigerator. Save the processing for when you get back. Humidity wreaks havoc with film and optical equipment—make every effort to keep your gear dry.

Dress for the climate. This generally means dress for hot, sunny days and cooler evenings. Avoid bright colors and tight-fitting clothing. Loose cotton clothing—preferably with lots of pockets— and sturdy, comfortable shoes are ideal. Be sure to bring good sunglasses, a wide-brimmed hat and sun-block lotion. Insect repellent is also a must.

A red-billed hornbill, photographed in Kenya.

The quills sticking out from the secretary bird's head give it its name.

The great spotted cuckoo can be seen in Kenya. Unlike most birds, cuckoos have two toes pointing forward and two pointing backward.

Kenya

The array of birds to be seen in Kenya is almost incredible. In a country that has set aside 10 percent of its land for national parks (equal in size to Switzerland), it is not unusual to spot more than 100 different birds in a single day. The rainy season in Kenya is between March and June; a shorter rainy season comes in November and early December. Many birders go to Kenya in November, when the migration period is at its peak. Below is a summary of the principal parks for birding.

Aberdares National Park and Mount Kenya National Park. The highland forests, bamboo groves and alpine moors of these parks make them good places to see thirteen species of sunbird, as well as green ibises, Jackson's francolins, white-headed wood hoopoes, silvery-cheeked hornbills, mustached green tinkerbirds and many others.

Samburu, Meru and Tsavo National Parks. All of these parks have rivers running through acacia bush and grasslands. The habitats are ideal for ostriches, vultures, a wide variety of starlings, weavers and waxbills, and such charmingly named birds as the pale-chanting goshawk and white-bellied go-away bird. Lake Jipe in Tsavo National Park is an excellent spot for large concentrations of waterbirds.

Masai Mara National Reserve. The 669 square miles (1,672 sq km) of rolling savannah here are Kenya's slice of the Serengeti plain that makes Tanzania famous. This area is best known for the annual migration of wildebeest, for rhinos and for hippos. Among the birds to be seen are secretary birds, numerous raptors, ground hornbills, lilac-breasted rollers, and many larks, pipits and widowbirds. In the riverine forest along the Mara and Talek rivers turacos, kingfishers, blue flycatchers, double-toothed barbets and even rare Pel's fishing owls are found.

Lake Bogoria National Reserve and Lake Nakuru National Park. The lakes at the southern end of the Rift Valley attract vast numbers of birds. Alkaline Lakes Nakuru and Bogoria are famed for the vast numbers of lesser flamingos that flock here to feed on the algae—a million or more may be present in November. At these lakes, in combination with fresh-water Lakes

Baringo and Naivasha, over 400 species, primarily waterbirds, can be seen, among them pelicans, cormorants, bitterns, herons, gallinules, kingfishers and many wintering waders and ducks.

Kakamega Forest. Birds found nowhere else in Kenya are seen here, in the easternmost extension of the vast central African rain forest. Some of the birds that are seen here include blue-headed bee-eaters, black-billed weavers, red-headed bluebills, black-and-white-casqued hornbills, and many species of greenbul.

Sokoke Forest. The lowland forests of the Kenya coast are home to green barbets, black-headed apalis, sunbirds and many native and visiting rarities.

Zimbabwe and Namibia

Southern Africa has an amazing array of habitats, ranging from the forests of the Eastern Highlands and Victoria Falls to grassy savannah and the desert of the Namib. March is a good time to see this part of Africa: both resident and visiting birds are at the peak of breeding activity.

Bunga Forest National Park. The misty valleys of the Eastern Highlands in Zimbabwe are a good place to see orange thrushes, red-faced crimsonwings, yellow-bellied sunbirds, Barratt's warblers and many others.

Zambezi River. The forest comes down to the edge of Zimbabwe's Zambezi River, providing a habitat for an astonishing variety of birds. Livingstone's flycatchers, southern carmine bee-eaters, green pigeons, brown-headed parrots, hornbills and several kinds of raptors can be seen. At night Scops, giant and spotted eagle owls, are present, as are nightjars. Also present is Victoria Falls—a sight that overwhelms even dedicated birders.

Etosha National Park. Located in Namibia, this park contains over thirty species of birds of prey, including Kori and Ludwig's bustards. Other birds to be seen include fiery-necked nightjars, bare-faced babblers and huge numbers of spotted sandgrouse. The dry regions of Etosha contain many kinds of lark, such as clapper, Stark's, Sabota and rufous-naped larks.

Namib Desert. The Namib Desert has little landbird life, but the seabirds are fascinating. Albatrosses, petrels, shearwaters and skuas can be seen offshore. On the coast, nest platforms have been erected to attract huge colonies of white pelicans, Bank cormorants and Cape cormorants; the guano is harvested for fertilizer. Many wading birds are found in the shallow pools near the platforms.

A colony of social weavers has taken over an acacia tree on the plains of Tanzania.

Ground hornbills can be seen in Kenya.

Attracted to a feeder, this speckled pigeon was photographed by Dr. Bill Hardy on a Holbrook Travel tour.

Carmine bee-eaters can be seen along the banks of the Zambesi River in Zimbabwe.

Tanzania

Tanzania in February is a birder's paradise—the rains are over and the birds are breeding. The premier spot is the Serengeti plain, but wonderful birding is also found at Ngorongoro Crater, Lake Manyara, Kilimanjaro, Tarangire National Park and Arusha National Park. On the plains ostriches, secretary birds and bustards are common. Bee-eaters, starlings, rollers, sunbirds, weavers and finches are everywhere, as are such typically African birds as honeyguides, wood hoopoes, larks and warblers. Unusual endemic birds such as Jackson's widowbirds, gray-breasted spurfowls and ashy starlings are also found.

Western Africa

The Ivory Coast, Senegal and Gambia on Africa's west coast are home to over a thousand species of birds, many of which are found nowhere else. The average birding trip to this region can easily add 400 birds to a life list.

Tunisia and Morocco

Virtually all the North African bird species can be seen on a trip combining Tunisia and Morocco. Even in the Sahara Desert of southern Tunisia there are thirteen species of lark, and migrants flock to the oases. Heading north, the terrain becomes more varied. Lake Ishkeul attracts many waterbirds, while at the saltwater lakes near the coast are gulls and shorebirds. During the peak period in March and April numerous migrants and raptors can be seen at Cap Bon on the coast.

The Moroccan Sahara is home to desert species such as thick-billed larks and coroneted sandgrouse. In the Atlas Mountains the endangered Waldrapp ibis can be found. The Sous valley is an excellent place to see migrating warblers.

Vulturine groundfowl in Kenya.

African Tourist Offices and Embassies

Ivory Coast
Ivory Coast Embassy
2424 Massachusetts Avenue, NW
Washington, DC   20008
(202) 483-2400

Kenya
Kenya Tourist Office
424 Madison Avenue
New York, NY   10017
(212) 486-1300

Embassy of Kenya
2249 R Street, NW
Washington, DC   20008
(202) 387-6101

Morocco
Embassy of Morocco
1601 21 Street, NW
Washington, DC   20007
(202) 462-7979

Consulate General of Morocco
437 Fifth Avenue
New York, NY   10016
(212) 758-2625

Moroccan National Tourist Office
20 East 46 Street
New York, NY 10017
(212) 557-2520

Senegal
Embassy of Senegal
2112 Wyoming Avenue, NW
Washington, DC   20008
(202) 234-0540

Tanzania
Embassy of Tanzania
2139 R Street, NW
Washington, DC   20008
(202) 939-6125

Tunisia
Embassy of Tunisia
1515 Massachusetts Avenue, NW
Washington, DC   20008
(202) 862-1850

ASIA

Planning for Asia

The countries of Asia are richly diverse. India, Japan, Borneo, Thailand, Malaysia, Indonesia are all part of Asia, yet they vary tremendously. As with a trip to any other exotic place, the services of professional birding tour operators are invaluable in Asia. Contact the tourist offices and embassies of the countries you plan to visit for further information—and be sure to ask about health hazards and visas. (For more advice on planning a successful trip, see page 204.)

India

India is rich in an astonishing array of bird life—nearly 1,300 species have been recorded on the subcontinent. Birds such as the Siberian rubythroat winter in India alongside the many amazing endemic birds. There are twenty-eight species of owl, seventeen of pheasant, and fourteen of colorful sunbird. On an average trip several hundred native species can be seen, as well as migrants. The best sites for bird-viewing are too numerous to list; below are just some highlights.

Sultanpur Jheel. About 100 species are easily seen at this large, shallow lake near Delhi. Among them are ring-necked parakeets, red-vented bulbuls, purple sunbirds, Indian rollers, black ibises, spotted eagles and Brook's leaf warblers.

Bharatpur. This freshwater swamp about two hours from Agra can provide up to 200 species of great diversity. Numerous waterbirds, including Siberian cranes, open-billed and painted storks, bar-headed geese, ferruginous ducks and red-crested pochards can all be seen. In the surrounding trees and bushes are yellow-legged green pigeons, paradise flycatchers, white-bellied drongos, coppersmith barbets, gray partridges, parakeets, Tickell's thrushes, Siberian rubythroats, and thick-billed

India is home to many fascinating endemic birds; numerous migrants are also seen.

warblers. Dusky eagle owls, mottled wood owls and jungle nightjars are active at dawn and dusk. October to January is the best time to visit.

The Himalayas. The western Himalayas at the borders of China and Nepal are at an elevation of over 20,000 feet (6,000 m) (roughly the height of Mt. McKinley, the highest mountain in North America). The unusual birds to be seen here include red-flanked bluetails, Himalayan greenfinches, Nepal rosefinches, velvet-fronted nuthatches, Himalayan griffon vultures, crossbeaks, bulbuls, titmice, great hill barbets and black-capped sibias.

Kaziranga National Park. Located in Assam, this little-known park is a good place to see Asian elephants, water buffaloes and one-horned rhinos, as well as spiderhunters, giant hornbills, tailorbirds, spot-billed pelicans, fairy bluebirds and many others. The best months are January to March.

Corbett National Park. This famous preserve in Uttar Pradesh was created as part of Project Tiger. While providing a refuge for these endangered animals, it has also become a prime birding spot. Since walking through tiger territory is more than a little hazardous, bird-watching at Corbett is done on elephantback! Among the birds to be seen this way are spangled drongos, orange-fronted leafbirds, pied kingfishers, gray-headed fishing eagles, giant hornbills, plumbeous redstarts, jungle owlets, wallcreepers and white-crested laughing thrushes. November to May are the best months to see the park.

A painted stork rests characteristically on one leg in India.

Flamingos preen on a lakeshore in India.

Long-toed stints can be found in the mangrove swamps fringing the Gulf of Siam in Thailand.

Thailand

The bird life in Thailand is extremely diverse, in part because the country covers three distinct habitats and in part because it is the winter destination of many migrants. For that reason, the best time to visit is during the winter months, when the climate is also cooler and drier. Among the 1,200 birds that can be seen here are some of the world's most beautiful.

Gulf of Siam. The mangrove swamps around the gulf are a gathering point for many shorebirds, including wintering waders. Birds to be seen here include oriental plovers, Nordmann's greenshanks, redshanks and long-toed stints.

Khao Yai National Park. This is the place for large forest birds such as hornbills, trogons, broadbills, woodpeckers, bulbuls, flycatchers, warblers, nightjars and sunbirds. Red jungle fowls are also present.

Doi Inthanon National Park. Located in the mountainous northern region of Thailand, this park and the area around Chiang Mai are good places to encounter many Himalayan birds. Those present include many passerines such as minivets, leafbirds, laughing thrushes, babblers and parrotbills. Many wintering warblers can be seen.

Well over a thousand bird species have been recorded in India, including these egrets.

Japanese cranes at Lake Furen on the island of Hokkaido.

Taman Negara National Park in Malaysia is a haven for red-bearded bee-eaters.

Japan

The islands of Japan range from flat in the south to alpine ruggedness and high elevations in the north. Over 500 species of birds are found in the varied habitats, including more than 200 breeding species.

Miyake. Miyakejima is considered the best birding spot in the Izu Islands. This is a good place to see endemic birds such as the Izu Islands thrush; Japanese robins and Middendorff's grasshopper warblers are among birds to be seen.

Mt. Noriukura and Kamikochi. The region around Mt. Noriukura in the Japanese Alps is extremely beautiful—and rich in birds. Among the montane species here are Japanese accentors, cuckoos, Siberian blue robins, Japanese yellow buntings, Japanese green woodpeckers, Japanese grosbeaks and many other interesting birds.

Shimokita Peninsula. At the northern tip of the island of Honshu, the Shimokita Peninsula has an abundance of marshes and rice paddies. Breeding great cormorants are among the wading birds to be found here.

Hokkaido. At Lake Furen on the island of Hokkaido are found three kinds of grasshopper warbler, six kinds of woodpecker, nesting slaty-backed gulls, Japanese cranes, buntings, spectacled guillemots and other birds. The extremely rare Blakiston's fish owl might be glimpsed. The Japanese Crane Sanctuary is here. Teuri Island off the coast has some very large seabird rookeries.

Sado Island. The Japanese crested ibis, a seriously endangered bird, can be seen on this island.

Malaysia

The lush tropical rain forest that covers most of peninsular Malaysia is home to over 600 resident birds, including many found only here. Taman Negara National Park is the prime place to see birds. Located in the center of the peninsula, the park covers over 1,600 square miles (4,200 sq km); over 350 species have been seen here. Crested firebacks, red-bearded bee-eaters, broadbills, babblers and many bulbuls are just some of the birds present. Elusive species such as the helmeted hornbill may also be seen. The many rain forest animals that are also seen are an added bonus.

Borneo

The forests of Borneo are extremely old, with a very rich diversity of plant and animal life found nowhere else. Kinabalu National Park in Borneo is a fantastic birding spot. The forested slopes of towering Mt. Kinabalu are home to a number of endemic species such as the Kinabalu friendly warbler. Crimson-headed wood partridges, mountain barbets, mountain wren-babblers and many other birds are found here.

Indonesia

The islands of Indonesia have an enormous array of tropical and endemic birds. Unfortunately, population pressures have led to the destruction of forest land, but many birds remain.

Java. The reserves at Ujung Kulon and Gunug Gede-Pangrango are good places to see barbets, bulbuls and babblers.

Bali. The very rare Rothschild's myna might be seen here.

Sulawesi. Long known as the Celebes, this island has seventy-eight endemic species of pigeons, parrots, kingfishers and mynas, among others.

Asian Tourist Offices and Embassies

India

Embassy of India
2107 Massachusetts Avenue, NW
Washington, DC   20008
(202) 939-7000

India Consulate General
3 East 64 Street
New York, NY   10021
(212) 879-7800

India Government Tourist Office
30 Rockefeller Plaza
New York, NY   10112
(212) 586-4901

Indonesia

Indonesian Embassy
2020 Massachusetts Avenue, NW
Washington, DC   20008
(202) 775-5200

Indonesian Consulate General and
    Information Office
5 East 68 Street
New York, NY   10021
(212) 879-0600

Indonesian Travel and Tourism
352 Seventh Avenue
New York, NY   10001
(212) 564-1939

Japan

Embassy of Japan
2520 Massachusetts Avenue, NW
Washington, DC   20008
(202) 939-6700

Consulate General of Japan
299 Park Avenue
New York, NY   10171
(212) 371-8222

Japan National Tourist Organization
630 Fifth Avenue
New York, NY   10111
(212) 757-5640

Malaysia

Embassy of Malaysia
2401 Massachusetts Avenue, NW
Washington, DC 20008
(202) 328-2700

Malaysian Tourist Center
420 Lexington Avenue
New York, NY   10017
(212) 697 8995

Thailand

Royal Thai Embassy
2300 Kalorama Road, NW
Washington, DC   20008
(202) 537-1936

Tourism Authority of Thailand
5 World Trade Center
New York, NY   10048
(212) 432-0433

AUSTRALIA, NEW ZEALAND AND PAPUA NEW GUINEA

Australia

Over 700 species of birds are found in Australia. Incredibly, over half are endemic, including emus, lyrebirds, and scrub birds. Birds found only in Australia and New Guinea include cassowaries, birds of paradise and bowerbirds. Parrots are found in great diversity, and unusual waterbirds are common. More than fifty kinds of honeyeater are found, as are many species of wren. The terrain of this island continent varies enormously, from the arid center to the tropical coast to mountain rain forest. Many preserves and national parks make Australia an excellent place for birdwatchers.

Australia is a long way from anywhere else, so leave plenty of time in the itinerary to recover from the long flight. Australia is also a very large, very empty place (14 million people in 3 million square miles [7.8 million sq km]), and distances between birding spots can be great. The average visitor can do no more than visit some of the highlights. So large is Australia that the cities mentioned below are just the closest populated centers—the actual birding sites can be several hours away.

Most flightless birds, like this Australian emu, rely on size, not flight, to protect themselves against predators.

The most remarkable feature of a cockatoo (a type of parrot) is its crest. Here a Major Mitchell's cockatoo, native to Australia, shows off.

Sydney. On the southeastern coast in New South Wales, Sydney is a good base for seeing pelagic birds of the Southern Hemisphere, including albatrosses, petrels and shearwaters.

Brisbane. Lamington National Park contains rain forest and eucalyptus forests. Pied butcherbirds, pale-headed and crimson rosellas, Australian brush turkeys, Australian king parrots, regent and silk bowerbirds and paradise riflebirds are some of the amazing birds here.

Melbourne. Phillip Island in Phillip Bay off Melbourne, on the southern coast facing Tasmania, is the home of nesting little penguins. Other birds in the Melbourne area include black-faced shags, hooded plovers, straw-necked ibises, bell miners and pink robins. The eucalyptus trees of Toolangi State Forest shelter lyrebirds and many other birds. In Wyperfield National Park well to the north of the city, emus, malleefowls, yellow-plumed honeyeaters and pink cockatoos can be seen.

Adelaide. This coastal region has many saltwater marshlands and a correspondingly large number of waterbirds, including banded stilts, musk ducks, marsh harriers and red-rumped parrots.

Alice Springs. In the McDonnell Ranges at the center of Australia, Alice Springs offers vast stretches of scrub country. Birds here and at Simpson's Gap National Park include variegated wrens, diamond doves, pink-eared ducks, hooded robins and crested bellbirds.

Ayers Rock. This incredible rock formation in the desert of western Australia is an excellent place for birdwatching. Numerous honeyeaters and thornbills can be seen; rare birds include the

Straw-necked ibises soar gracefully through the Australian sky.

chiming wedgebill and crimson chat.

Darwin. The coastal area of the Northern Territory offers many birds, including red-winged parrots, mangrove robins, rainbow pittas and blue-winged kookaburras. Vast numbers of waterbirds are found, including many unusual herons, egrets, wading birds and ducks.

Atherton Tablelands. The amazing birdlife in the tropical rain forests and along the coast of this part of Queensland is matched only by the teeming life of the nearby Great Barrier Reef. Waterbirds seen along the shore near Cairns include herons, ibises, cormorants, waders and pelicans. In the forests are spotted harriers, golden bowerbirds, gray-headed robins, buff-banded rails, forest kingfishers and Victoria's riflebirds, among others. The coral islands of the Great Barrier Reef support colonies of nesting sooty terns and common noddies; brown boobies, frigatebirds and black-naped terns are also seen.

Australian Birding

A birdwatching holiday in Australia is an adventure to be enjoyed. Two good places providing accommodations and field guides are:

Cassowary House
Black Mountain Road
Box 252
Kuranda
Queensland   4872

Gipsy Point Lodge
Gipsy Point
Victoria   3889

The gray-headed robin of Australia is not a member of the thrush family; it is a type of flycatcher.

New Zealand

Many endangered birds are found in New Zealand, including black stilts and stitchbirds. Forty endemic birds are found here, as well as astonishing numbers of breeding seabirds, including three species of penguin, prions, petrels, shearwaters and several albatrosses.

Some of the world's most beautiful scenery is also found here, punctuated by unusual geothermal sites. New Zealand never really gets hot and has no dry season. In the late spring and summer, the warmest times of the year, daytime high temperatures average between 65 and 75°F (18 and 24°C).

North Island. The islands of the Hauraki Gulf near Auckland offer bellbirds, red-crowned parakeets, gannets, little blue penguins, petrels, arctic skuas, white-fronted terns, brown kiwis, riflemans, stitchbirds, tuis, saddlebacks, kokakos and kakapos. The Coromandel Peninsula has numerous tidal estuaries

The symbol of New Zealand is the kiwi, a flightless bird.

that harbor New Zealand dotterels, white-faced and red herons, pied stilts, fernbirds and banded rails and many coastal birds. Near the geysers and hot springs of Rotorua, bellbirds, tuis, whiteheads, gray warblers, riflemans, fantails, gulls, shags and scaups can be found. In the Lake Taupo region bitterns and dabchicks are common; scaups, black swans, spotless crakes and fernbirds are also found. In nearby Pureora Forest Park there are falcons, kakas, parakeets, pigeons, whiteheads, riflemans, robins, fantails, bellbirds and tuis.

South Island. The subalpine region of Mt. Cook National Park is a fine place to see New Zealand falcons. The Catlin Forest Park is an excellent place to see coastal birds, including yellow-eyed penguins, the world's rarest. The Eglinton Valley and Lake Gunn offer bellbirds, gray warblers, robins, yellowheads, parakeets, fantails, tomtits, brown creepers and finches.

Stewart Island. This small island is perhaps the finest birding area in all of New Zealand. Wandering, royal and light-mantled sooty albatrosses; diving, giant and Cook's petrels; fairy and broad-billed prions; Buller's and shy mollymants; sooty shearwaters and crested, yellow-eyed and little blue penguins can all be seen. Numerous shags and oystercatchers are also found along the coast. In the interior, bellbirds, parakeets, brown creepers, yellow-breasted tits and many other birds are found.

This tui was photographed near Rotorua on the North Island of New Zealand.

The charming little blue penguin is found on the North Island of New Zealand.

Papua New Guinea

New Guinea is the second-largest island in the world, and has an incredibly diverse bird life. Over 700 species are found; nearly half are endemic. The thirty-three different birds of paradise are probably best known, but there are also cassowaries, parrots, kingfishers, bowerbirds, mound builders and fairy-wrens. The many fabulous butterflies are almost as interesting as the birds. The terrain of New Guinea is still largely wilderness and includes extensive cloud forest in the southern highlands. In the south is the Bensbach, a vast area of lowland savannahs, home to huge numbers of breeding waterbirds. Papua New Guinea is popularly thought to be a land of steamy jungles. This is true in places, but in other areas the climate is surprisingly pleasant.

Tourist Information

Australia
Embassy of Australia
Washington, DC   20008
(202) 797-3000

Australian Consulate General
636 Fifth Avenue
New York, NY   10020
(212) 245-4000

Australian Tourist Commission
489 Fifth Avenue
New York, NY   10017
(212) 687-6300

New Zealand
New Zealand Embassy
Washington, DC   20008
(202) 328-4800

New Zealand Consulate General
630 Fifth Avenue
New York, NY   10111
(212) 586-0060

New Zealand Tourist and Publicity
*   Office*
10960 Wilshire Boulevard
Los Angeles, CA   90024
(213) 477-8241

Papua New Guinea
Embassy of Papua New Guinea
1330 Connecticut Avenue, NW
Washington, DC   20008
(202) 659-0856

New Zealand has many unusual flightless birds, including this weka, found on North Island.

The blue-winged kookaburra is one of Australia's many unusual birds.

TOURS FOR BIRDERS

A number of companies offer excellent tours designed specifically for birders. Usually led by experienced professional ornithologists, such tours are carefully planned to coincide with the peak viewing periods at the destination. The groups are small, generally no more than twenty people and often fewer. Bird tours are not quite the same as other organized travel. Because the trips are often to places off the beaten track, weather delays and itinerary changes at the last moment are possible. The schedule is a bit different too: birds are most active early in the morning, and so are tour members. Expect to be on the move quite a bit during the day. By evening most tour members are ready to skip the local nightlife in favor of bed, which is just as well, since there often isn't a lot of nightlife in say, Amazonian Peru.

The list below presents a number of highly regarded companies offering birding tours in North America and around the world. All will provide free catalogs with extensive tour descriptions.

International (including North America)

American Museum of Natural History Discovery Tours
Central Park West at 79 Street
New York, NY 10024
(800) 462-8687/(212) 769-5700

Cheesemans' Ecology Safaris
20800 Kittredge Road
Saratoga, CA 95070
(408) 867-1371/(408) 741-5330

Field Guides Incorporated
Box 160723
Austin, TX 78746
(512) 327-4953

Holbrook Travel, Inc.
3540 N.W. 13 Street
Gainesville, FL 32609
(904) 377-7111

International Zoological Expeditions, Inc.
210 Washington Street
Sherborn, MA 01770
(617) 655-1461

Joseph Van Os Nature Tours
Box 655
Vashon Island, WA 98070
(206) 463-5383

Massachusetts Audubon Society
Tour Director, Conservation Department
Lincoln, MA 01773
(617) 259-9500

McHugh Ornithology Tours
101 West Upland Road
Ithaca, NY 14850
(607) 257-7829

National Audubon Society Travel
950 Third Avenue
New York, NY 10022
(212) 546-9140

Questers Tour and Travel, Inc.
257 Park Avenue South
New York, NY 10010
(212) 673-3120

Raptours
Box 8008
Silver Spring, MD 20907
(301) 565-9196

Society Expeditions
3131 Elliott Avenue, Suite 700
Seattle, WA 98121
(800) 426-7794/(206) 285-9400

Victor Emanuel Nature Tours, Inc.
Box 33008
Austin, TX 78764
(512) 328-5221

Wings, Inc.
Box 31930
Tucson, AZ 85751
(602) 749-1967

Woodstar Tours Inc.
908 South Massachusetts Avenue
De Land, FL 32724
(904) 736-0327

Central and South America

Turtle Tours
25 East 51 Street
New York, NY 10022
(212) 355-1404

Asia

InnerAsia Expeditions
2627 Lombard Street
San Francisco, CA 94123
(800) 551-1769/(415) 922-0448

King Bird Tours
Box 196
Planetarium Station
New York, NY 10024
(212) 866-7923

Australia, New Zealand and the South Pacific

Cassowary Tours
Box 252 Kuranda
Queensland 4872
Australia

Goanna Tour
55 Guide Street
Clifton Beach 4871
Australia

Monarch Australian Birding Tours
SH Enterprises
14252 Culver Drive
Irvine, CA 92714
(714) 733-1744

Pacific Exploration Company
Box 3042
Santa Barbara, CA 93130
(805) 687-7282

Africa

Park East Tours, Inc.
1841 Broadway
New York, NY 10023
(800) 223-6078/(212) 765-4870

Peregrine Tours
Box 4251
Seattle WA 98104
(206) 767-9937

A regent bowerbird inside his elaborately constructed bower, designed to catch the eye of an interested female.

6
GETTING SERIOUS

Bird Banding • Courses and Expeditions • Libraries • Bird Observatories • Bird Taxonomy

BIRD BANDING

Bird banding in America began with John James Audubon around 1803. Audubon tied silver wires around the legs of a brood of fledgling phoebes; two returned to the same place the following year. Modern, scientific banding, however, really began in 1890 with a Danish schoolteacher named Hans Christian Mortenson. Over several years Mortenson placed bands marked with his name and address on teals, pintails, storks, starlings and hawks. Soon he was receiving reports from all over Europe, and other bird lovers began to follow his example. The interest in "ringing," as it is called in Europe, soon spread to the United States. The American Bird Banding Association was founded in 1909. World War I caused the group's work to lag, however, and in 1920 the Bureau of Biological Survey (now the U.S. Fish and Wildlife Service) joined with its northern counterpart, the Canadian Wildlife Service, to take over the association's work.

Bird banding data collected since then has been a crucial source of information about the lives of individual birds as well as species. Bird banding has proved that wild birds often live ten years or longer. For example, a black duck banded on Cape Cod was taken by a hunter seventeen years later in Newfoundland; a red-winged blackbird banded in New York was found fourteen years later in North Carolina. The American longevity record of thirty-six years was established by a herring gull banded off the coast of Maine in 1930 while still a nestling and found dead along the shore of northern Lake Michigan in 1966. Bird banding provides important information about migration and migration routes. Banding has shown that some birds, such as the golden plover, do not return north in the spring over the same route they took in the fall. Bands returned from such faraway places as France, Nigeria and South Africa helped demonstrate the remarkable migration pattern of the arctic tern, proving that this bird makes an annual round-trip flight of 25,000 miles (40,000 km) from its nesting grounds near the Arctic Circle to its wintering grounds in Antarctica.

A male black and white warbler is banded during the spring migration at Long Point Bird Observatory.

Zack Klyver and Bill Clark of the Institute for Field Ornithology make their observations of a male merlin.

How Birds Are Banded

Specially designed nets and traps are used to catch birds for banding. Extreme care is taken by the banders to avoid injuring the bird in any way. Trapped birds are removed and identified and examined for age, sex and physical condition. An aluminum band of the appropriate size is attached to the bird's leg and the bird is released.

Authorized banders receive bands and reporting forms without charge from the Bird Banding Laboratory. When the band is attached the bander records the number, the kind of bird, its age and sex, and the place and date of banding. This information is returned to the Bird Banding Laboratory, where it is stored in a computer. The data base contains entries on well over 40 million bird bands, with about a million new entries made every year. In the years since 1920 there been nearly three million verified returns, an average of 45,000 to 60,000 every year. Some 97 percent of all the birds banded are never found again, but the information provided by those that are is invaluable. Very small birds are the least likely to be seen again, while up to 10 percent of banded gamebirds may be recovered.

Becoming a Bird Bander

More than half of the 2,500 master banders are dedicated amateur ornithologists involved with nongame bird banding studies. Anyone who is at least eighteen years of age and can identify all of the common birds in their different seasonal plumages may apply for a banding permit from the Fish and Wildlife Service or the Canadian Wildlife Service. The applicant must furnish the names of three well-known bird banders or ornithologists who can vouch for his or her fitness as a bird bander. Only those persons who are well qualified and wish to assist with research projects are issued banding permits.

If You Find a Banded Bird

Banded game birds shot by hunters are the most likely to be reported back to the Bird Banding Laboratory. Dead birds found anywhere, but especially along highways and seashores, may carry bands. The bands are not always found on the birds, however. Occasionally one is found in a fish stomach, and some are found in owl pellets and in the nests of birds of prey.

If you find a band on a dead bird, remove it and straighten it out. A serial number and the words "ADVISE BIRD BAND WRITE WASHINGTON, D.C. USA" can be seen. Tape the band securely to a piece of writing paper and list as much of the following information as possible:

1. *Your name and address.*
2. *All numbers and letters on the band*
3. *The date you found the band*
4. *The place where you found the band. Include the mileage and direction from the nearest town and list the county and state.*
5. *Describe how you found the band. For example, was the bird found dead? Was it shot by a hunter?*

Place the letter in an envelope, mark the envelope "Hand Cancel" (bird bands play havoc with mail-sorting machines) and mail it to:

Bird Banding Laboratory
U.S. Fish and Wildlife Service
Laurel, MD 20708

If you find a band on a living bird, *do not* attempt to remove it—you might injure the bird. Carefully note the number on the band and release the bird. If it is ever noted again, the band will provide valuable information about the bird's life and travels. Send as much information as you can about the encounter to the Bird Banding Laboratory. Note: if the bird is very tiny, there is only room for the serial number on the outside of the band.

If you send in a band, you will receive a certificate of appreciation from the Bird Banding Laboratory telling you where the bird was banded, what kind it was and who banded it. The bander will also be told where and when you found the band.

The Bird Banding Mailbag

The Bird Banding Laboratory receives some 60,000 band recovery reports a year. Some are from hunters who are afraid they have murdered United States government property; others hope they will receive a reward. Sometimes people mail in the whole bird. This letter was received in 1982 from Cheng Jin-Fa of the People's Republic of China:

I feel very glad to wrote you. I did not know you and you did not know me. Who introduced I to you? It is your pigeon. SHE FLEW TO CHINA! What a far way she flew! It is marvelous!

In fact, the bird was a pintail duck that had been banded in Louisiana in 1978.

A legendary tale told at the Bird Banding Laboratory dates back to the time when it was called the Bureau of Biological Survey. A typographical error resulted in bird bands that read "Boil. Surv. Wash. D.C." A crow with one of these bands was shot by a farmer in Kansas, who supposedly wrote:

Dear Sirs, I am reporting a crow I shot wearing a metal band numbered 12694. I should report that I followed instructions on the band, but am badly disappointed in the result. I washed, boiled and surved, but the durned thing still wasn't fit to eat.

Removing a bird from the mist net that captured it for banding.

Bird Banding Organizations

Eastern Bird Banding Association
c/o Donald Mease
RD 2, Box 436A
Hellertown, PA   18055

Inland Bird Banding Association
c/o C. Holmes Smith
6305 Cumberland Road, SW
Sherrodsville, OH   44675

Western Bird Banding Association
c/o Dr. Howard L. Cogswell
1548 East Avenue
Hayward, CA   94541

Each organization publishes its own newsletter as well contributing jointly to the quarterly journal *North American Bird Bander.*

Placing a band on a bird's leg. The process is painless; careful handling minimizes the stress to the bird.

COURSES AND EXPEDITIONS

Courses

It's fairly easy to acquire a basic working knowledge of common birds—all that's needed is a good field guide. To go beyond that on your own, however, can involve a lot of time and frustration. A simpler and more enjoyable way of learning to distinguish fall warblers, for example, is to go on a warbler walk with members of your local bird club or National Audubon Society chapter. In addition to sponsoring walks, field trips, forays and the like, many bird organizations also offer lectures and slide talks in the evenings. The programs listed below are for those who want more specialized or advanced information.

Audubon Ecology Camps and Workshops
National Audubon Society
613 Riversville Road
Greenwich, CT 06831
(203) 869-2017

For more than fifty years the National Audubon Society has conducted camps and workshops in several locations across the country. Of particular interest to birders are the six-day Field Ornithology Workshops offered in late summer in Maine.

Seminars in Ornithology
Home Study Course in Bird Photography
Cornell Laboratory of Ornithology
159 Sapsucker Woods Road
Ithaca, NY 14850
(607) 256-5056

Seminars in Ornithology. This famous home study course in bird biology is at the level of an introductory college course in ornithology. Written by leading ornithologists and lavishly illustrated by well-known artists, the nine-lesson series is designed to be studied at the student's own pace. When ready, the student answers the questions for each lesson and sends them to an instructor at the laboratory for grading; the instructor is also available to answer any queries. Upon completion of the seminars, the student is awarded a certificate.

Home Study Course in Bird Photography. This four-part course encourages the development of knowledge, skill and sensitivity through a comprehensive, heavily illustrated text, a set of study slides and critiques of the student's

Visitors to the Point Reyes Bird Observatory's Palomarin Landbird Research Station get a close look at a song sparrow.

Students at the Institute for Field Ornithology set up for an observation session on Deer Island, New Brunswick.

The Long Point Bird Observatory in Port Rowan, Ontario uses this tower for observation.

photos by an instructor at the laboratory. Topics covered include selecting and using equipment, photographing birds in flight, remote-control photography, photographing birds at the nest and more. To receive a graduation certificate, students must complete the course work and four special assignments—a process that usually takes nine months to a year.

The Institute for Field Ornithology
University of Maine at Machias
9 O'Brien Avenue
Machias, ME   04654
(207) 255-3313

The courses offered through the non-profit Institute for Field Ornithology (founded in 1983) take place not only at the University of Maine campus at Machias on the coast of Maine but also in the Pacific Northwest, Colorado, Mexico and New Jersey. Recent workshops have included bird population studies (in conjunction with the Cornell Laboratory of Ornithology), warblers, raptors at Cape May Point, seabirds of the North Pacific and seabirds of the North Atlantic. Those attending the week-long workshops range from eager beginners to students receiving college credit to experienced professionals. All participate in a combination of class-room discussion and fieldwork taught by experienced ornithology instructors. The goal is always to improve birding skills and to increase cooperation between birdwatchers and professional ornithologists.

The Academy of Natural Sciences of
Philadelphia
Maine Island Ecology
19th and the Parkway, Logan Square
Philadelphia, PA   19103
(215) 299-1100

The Maine Island Ecology program is for high-school students with a genuine interest in ecological and environmental studies. The program, which has been in operation since 1970, is not specifically for birdwatchers, but ornithology is taught as part of the overall approach to ecology. Most of the time is spent in fieldwork requiring the active participation of every student; there is little classroom work. As part of the two-week program each student chooses and conducts a study project that becomes a part of the permanent library. The program takes place at the Hardwood Island Biological Station in Mount Desert, Maine. The offshore island can be reached only by boat; there is no electricity or telephone. The station is extremely well equipped, with an excellent laboratory and library and comfortable living quarters.

Expeditions

An interesting way of combining a vacation with a learning experience (and sometimes a tax deduction) is to volunteer for an expedition. Although this unusual route can be a relatively inexpensive way to see some exotic places, it is not for luxury lovers—accommodations are often simply tents in the field a long way from anywhere, volunteers are expected to work—and it is not free. However, being a volunteer on a serious research project is highly educational and very satisfying. The organizations listed below bring expedition organizers and volunteers together.

Earthwatch
680 Mt. Auburn Street
Watertown, MA   02272
(617) 926-8200

International Research Expeditions
140 University Drive
Menlo Park, CA   94205
(415) 323-4228

Great Plains Wildlife Research
Institute
Box 297
Casper, WY   82602
(307) 265-3731

LIBRARIES

A number of special libraries at universities, museums and organizations are open to the public for research. This is an excellent way to look at hard-to-find or rare birding volumes. Since most libraries subscribe to all the birding journals, it is also a good way to look up interesting articles in back issues. In most cases, the books and journals about birds are part of a larger library of natural history. Contact the library in advance to check on the hours and to arrange permission to visit.

United States

Natural History Museum of Los Angeles County
Research Library
900 Exposition Boulevard
Los Angeles, CA   90007
(213) 744-3387

Hartnell Community College
O.P. Silliman Memorial Library
156 Homestead Avenue
Salinas, CA   93901
(408) 755-6870

Denver Museum of Natural History
Library
City Park
Denver, CO   80205
(303) 575-3610

United States Department of
Agriculture
Denver Wildlife Research Center
Library
Federal Center, Building 16
Box 25266
Denver, CO   80225
(303) 326-7873

Trinity College
Watkinson Library
300 Summit Street
Hartford, CT   06106
(203) 527-3151

Yale University
Ornithology Library
Peabody Museum
170 Whitney Avenue
New Haven, CT   06511
(203) 432-3793

Smithsonian Institution
National Museum of Natural
History Library
Natural History Building
10th and Constitution Avenue
Washington, DC   20560
(202) 357-1496

Smithsonian Institution Libraries
Special Collections Branch
MAH 5016
Washington, DC   20560
(202) 357-1568

Wetmore Ornithology Collection
United States Fish and Wildlife Service
Office of Audiovisual Services Library
Department of the Interior, Room 8070
Washington, DC   20240
(202) 343-8770

United States National Park Service
Everglades National Park Reference
*   Library*
Box 279
Homestead, FL   33030
(305) 245-5266

Field Museum of Natural History
Library
Roosevelt Road and Lake Shore Drive
Chicago, IL   60605
(312) 922-9410

The annual hawk watch at New Jersey Audubon's Cape May Bird Observatory.

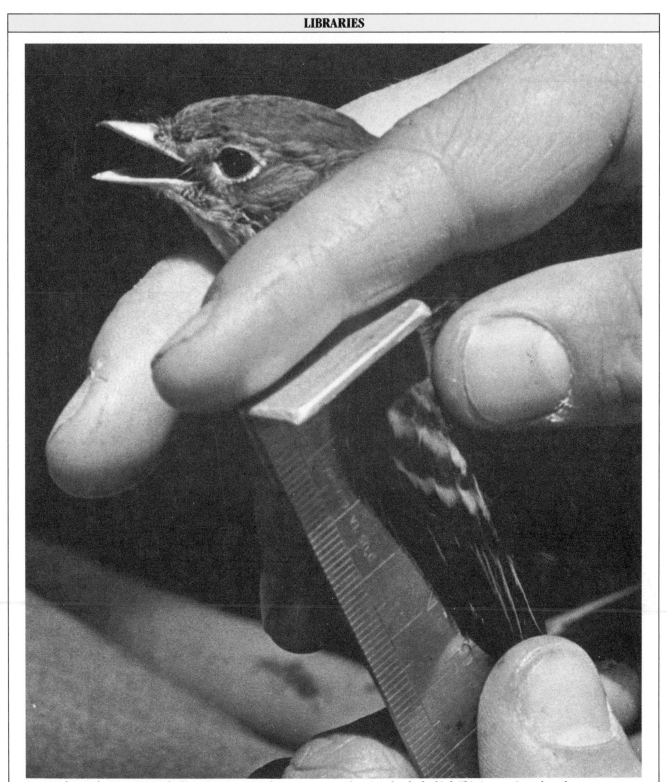

A researcher at the Manomet Bird Observatory in Massachusetts measures the wing chord of a bird. This is sometimes the only way to recognize certain hard-to-identify species.

Ayer Ornithology Library
Illinois State Museum of Natural History
   and Art
Technical Library
Springfield, IL   62706
(217) 782-6623

R.M. Barnes ornithology collection
University of Kansas
Department of Special Collections
Spencer Research Library
Lawrence, KS   66045
(913) 864-4334
History of Ornithology

**Natural History Society of Maryland
Library**
2643 North Charles Street
Baltimore, MD   21218
(301) 235-6116

**United States Fish and Wildlife
Service**
**Patuxent Wildlife Research Center
Library**
Laurel, MD   20708
(301) 498-0235

**University of Massachusetts,
Amherst**
**Biological and Geological Sciences
Library**
214 Morrill Science Center
Amherst, MA   01003
(413) 545-2674

**Arthur Cleveland Bent Ornithology
Collection**
Manomet Bird Observatory Library
Box 936
Manomet, MA   02345
(617) 224-6521

Josselyn Van Tyne Memorial Library
University of Michigan Museum of
   Zoology
Ann Arbor, MI   48109

**Library of the Wilson Ornithological
Society**
University of Michigan
Natural Science Library
3140 Natural Science Building
Ann Arbor, MI   48109
(313) 764-1494

The observation tower at the Whitefish Point Bird Observatory in Michigan.

Michigan Audubon Society
Edith Munger Library
409 West E Avenue
Kalamazoo, MI   49007
(616) 344-8648

University of Minnesota
**Bell Museum of Natural History
Library**
10 Church Street, SE
Minneapolis, MN   55455
(612) 624-1639

Cornell University
History of Science Collections
215 Olin Research Library
Ithaca, NY   14853
(607) 255-4033

**Hill Collection of 18th- and 19th-
century North American ornithology**
Cornell University
Laboratory of Ornithology Library
159 Sapsucker Woods Road
Ithaca, NY   14850
(607) 255-5565

Cornell University
**Laboratory of Ornithology Library
of Natural Sounds**
159 Sapsucker Woods Road
Ithaca, NY   14850
(607) 255-4035
60,000 sound recordings

**American Museum of Natural
History**
Department of Library Services
Central Park West at 79th Street
New York, NY   10024
(212) 769-5000

United States Fish and Wildlife Service
Northern Prairie Wildlife Research Center Library
Box 2096
Jamestown, ND   58402
(701) 252-5363

Carnegie Museum of Natural History Library
4400 Forbes Avenue
Pittsburgh, PA   15213
(412) 622-3264

W.E. Clyde Todd Ornithological Reprint Collection, John P. Robin Library, G. Bernard Van Cleve Library
Texas A&M University
Special Collections Division
Sterling C. Evans Library
College Station, TX   77843
(409) 845-1951

Seattle Public Library
Business and Science Department
1000 Fourth Avenue
Seattle, WA   98104
(206) 625-2665

Canada

Environment Canada, Conservation and Protection
Western and Northern Region Library
4999 98 Avenue, Second floor
Edmonton, Alberta   T6B 2X3
(403) 425-5891

National Museums of Canada
Library Services Directorate
Ottawa, Ontario   K1A 0M8
(613) 998-3923

R.M. Anderson Collection
McGill University
Blacker/Wood Library of Zoology and
    Ornithology
Redpath Library Building
3459 McTavish Street
Montreal, Quebec   H3A 1Y1
(514) 392-4955

Environment Canada, Conservation and Protection
Canadian Wildlife Service
Quebec Region Library
1141 Route de l'Eglise
Box 10100
Ste. Foy, Quebec   G1V 4H5
(418) 648-7062

Environment Canada, Conservation and Protection
Canadian Wildlife Service
Prairie Migratory Bird Research Centre
    Library
115 Perimeter Road
Saskatoon, Saskatchewan   S7N OX4
(306) 975-4087

A researcher conducts a waterbird count at Whitefish Point Bird Observatory.

BIRD OBSERVATORIES

The principal activity of most bird observatories is the scientific study of migration through banding operations. For that reason, observatories are located at strategic coastal points along migration routes where both water and land birds can be found. Observatories provide valuable data and conduct their own ongoing research programs.

The Cape May Bird Observatory in Cape May, New Jersey, is funded by the New Jersey Audubon Society. The CMBO has been conducting raptor research since its founding in 1976. Ongoing programs study passerine birds and bird life around the shores of Delaware Bay. Specific research programs include winter bald eagle surveys, breeding northern harrier and short-eared owl surveys, nocturnal migration of owls at Cape May Point and colonial nesting bird surveys. Banding programs and demonstrations at CMBO have attracted thousands of visitors.

At the Long Point Bird Observatory in Ontario, Canada, intensive migration monitoring has been taking place since 1960, using the talents of hundreds of volunteers under the direction of a small core staff. Another very successful ongoing program is Project Feederwatch, now managed jointly by LPBO and Cornell University (see page 72 for more information about this). Many volunteers participate in the ongoing Ontario Lakes Loon Survey, which studies the effects of human disturbance and acid rain on the common loon population of Ontario. Visitors can stay at the two remote (access by boat only) field stations the observatory operates at Long Point; reservations at each station are on a first come, first served basis.

Point Reyes Bird Observatory in California is the oldest in America. The important research work of this private, nonprofit group is supported by contracts from agencies such as the National Science Foundation and also by private, corporate and foundation grants and gifts. Since 1964, PRBO has steadily expanded its three research areas (land birds, coastal and estuarine birds and marine birds) and carried out long-term biomonitoring of natural systems. Study areas range from the Farallon Islands to the high Sierras, and from the tropical Pacific to Antarctica. At the observatory's Landbird Research Station at Palomarin, at the southern portion of Point Reyes National Seashore, visitors can view bird-banding close up and talk with the field biologists.

The Whitefish Point Bird Observatory in Michigan was founded in 1976. In addition to extensive banding activities, one of the cornerstones of the observatory is the annual spring raptor count. Other ongoing programs include the spring waterbird migration count, an annual loon count, breeding bird studies and an owl-banding project.

A researcher gives a hawk talk to visitors at the Cape May Bird Observatory.

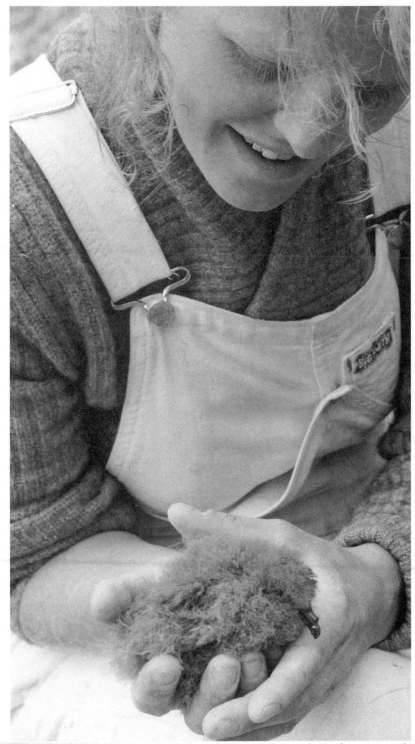

A researcher from the Point Reyes Bird Observatory prepares to weigh an ashy storm petrel chick on the Farallon Islands.

North American Bird Observatories

Point Reyes Bird Observatory
4990 State Route
Stinson Beach, CA   94970

San Francisco Bay Bird Observatory
Box 247
Alviso, CA   95002

Golden Gate Raptor Observatory
42 Glen Drive
Mill Valley, CA   94941

Manomet Bird Observatory
Box 936
Manomet, MA   02345

Whitefish Point Bird Observatory
c/o Rose Lake WRC
8562 East Stoll Road
East Lansing, MI   48823

Raccoon Ridge Bird Observatory
Box 1215 High Point
Montague, NJ   07827

Cape May Bird Observatory
New Jersey Audubon Society
Box 3
Cape May Point, NJ   08212

Long Point Bird Observatory
Box 160
Port Rowan, Ontario   N0E 1M0

A great gray owl is banded as part of an ongoing owl research program at Whitefish Point Bird Observatory.

A raptor count underway at Whitefish Point Bird Observatory.

Volunteers at the Great Plains Wildlife Research Institute band a pelican—carefully.

BIRD TAXONOMY

Taxonomy means the classification of living things by their degree of common characteristics, starting with the broadest categories and working down to the narrowest. Ornithologists classify birds mainly by such physical characteristics as bills, plumage and feet, as well as some more specialized traits. Thus, from a taxonomist's point of view, all feathered, winged, egg-laying animals are members of the class Aves of the phylum Chordata and the subphylum Vertebrata. All known birds fall into the subclass Neornithes. Within the subclass, all living (and some fossil) birds fall into the superorder Neognathae—which means birds with no teeth.

Within the subclass, birds are divided into orders, suborders, families and species. For all practical purposes, birdwatchers are chiefly concerned with orders (Latin suffix *-formes)*, families (Latin suffix *-dae*) and species (common name). The list below presents the major North American orders and families. Worldwide, there are twenty-eight living orders and over 9,000 species.

Order	Family	Common Family Name
Gaviiformes	*Gaviidae*	loons
Podicipediformes	*Podicipedidae*	grebes
Procellariiformes	*Procellariidae*	shearwaters, petrels
	Hydrobatidae	storm petrels
Pelecaniformes	*Phaethontidae*	tropicbirds
	Pelecanidae	pelicans
	Sulidae	boobies, gannets
	Phalacrocora-cidae	cormorants
	Anhingidae	anhingas
	Fregatidae	frigatebirds
Ciconiiformes	*Ardeidae*	bitterns, herons, egrets
	Ciconiidae	storks
	Threskiornithidae	ibises, spoonbills
Phoenicopter-iformes	*Phoenicopteridae*	flamingos
Anseriformes	*Anatidae*	waterfowl, including ducks, mergansers, swans, geese
Falconiformes	*Cathartidae*	vultures
	Accipitridae	hawks, including kites and eagles
	Pandionidae	ospreys
	Falconidae	falcons, kestrels
Galliformes	*Tetraonidae*	grouse
	Phasianidae	quails
	Meleagrididae	turkeys
Gruiformes	*Gruidae*	cranes
	Aramidae	limpkins
	Rallidae	rails, gallinules, coots
Charadriiformes	*Haematopodidae*	oystercatchers
	Recurvirostridae	avocets, stilts
	Charadriidae	plovers
	Scolopacidae	sandpipers
	Stercorariidae	jaegars, skuas
	Laridae	gulls, terns
	Rynchopidae	skimmers
	Alcidae	auks, puffins, murres
Columbiformes	*Columbidae*	pigeons, doves
Psittaciformes	*Psittacidae*	parrots
Cuculiformes	*Cuculidae*	cuckoos, roadrunners
Strigiformes	*Tytonidae*	barn owls
	Strigidae	other owls
Caprimulgi-formes	*Caprimulgidae*	goatsuckers
Apodiformes	*Apodidae*	swifts
	Trochilidae	hummingbirds

BIRD TAXONOMY

Order	Family	Common Family Name
Coraciiformes	*Alcedinidae*	kingfishers
Piciformes	*Picidae*	woodpeckers
Passeriformes	*Tyrannidae*	flycatchers
	Alaudidae	larks
	Hirundinidae	swallows
	Corvidae	crows, jays
	Paridae	titmice
	Sittidae	nuthatches
	Certhiidae	creepers
	Pycnonotidae	bulbuls
	Troglodytidae	wrens
	Mimidae	mockingbirds, thrashers
	Muscicapidae	kinglets, thrushes
	Motacillidae	pipits
	Bombycillidae	waxwings
	Laniidae	shrikes
	Sturnidae	starlings
	Vireonidae	vireos
	Emberizidae	warblers, tanagers, grosbeaks, buntings, sparrows, blackbirds, meadowlarks, orioles
	Fringillidae	finches
	Passeridae	weaver finches

Index

Numbers in italics indicate illustrations.

Photo Credits

Apostle Islands National Lakeshore: 166
Artwell Publishing: 96 top
Aspects, Inc.: 40 bottom, 44 bottom, 45, 113 top left and right
Austrian National Tourist Office: 192, 193
Belgian Tourist Office: 194
Big Bend National Park: 139, 140, 145 top, 147
Big Thicket National Preserve: 141 top, 157 top
Birder's Buddy: 17
Biscayne National Park: 8 top left, 81 top, 145 bottom, 148, 158, 159, 160 all, 161
Edward Marshall Boehm, Inc.: 117 top left and right, 118 top
Bogen Photo Corp.: 26 top and bottom
Borrobol Birding: 132, 196 bottom
Brazilian Tourism Foundation: 183, 184, 185, 189
British Tourist Authority: 196 top left and right
BushHawk: 27 bottom
Bushnell Division of Bausch & Lomb: 18 bottom
Canaveral National Seashore: 162 top and bottom
Canon U.S.A., Inc.: 24 (1, 3, 4, 5)
Cape May Bird Observatory: 238, 242
Carlson Images: 113 bottom
Celestron: 21 all, 23 bottom
Chiricahua National Monument: 135 top, 138
Cockerum Oregon Insects: 43
Cornell University Laboratory of Ornithology: 68 top and bottom, 69 top, 73
Department of Development and Tourism, Newfoundland/Labrador: 168 top, 169, 170, 171
Droll Yankees, Inc.: 36 top, 38, 49
Duncraft/Eileen Schlagenhaft: 39, 42, 44, 48, 50, 51, 55 top and bottom, 56 bottom, 61; S. Dunn: 40 top; 56 top left and right
Everglades National Park: 152
Russell A. Fink Gallery: 96 bottom, 97, 103
Fire Island National Seashore: 4 top, 6, 8 bottom, 13 top, 150 bottom, 164 all, 165 top and bottom
French West Indies Tourist Board: 190
Government of India Tourist Office: 212, 213, 214 top, 215
Government of Ontario Ministry of Tourism and Recreation: 167
Great Plains Wildlife Research Institute: 245 bottom
The Greenwich Workshop: 108

Gulf Islands National Seashore: 151, 153 bottom
The Hamilton Group: 116 top, 118 bottom, 119 bottom
Holbrook Travel/Dr. Bill Hardy: 180 top and bottom; 181 top and bottom, 182 top and bottom, 204, 208 top and bottom, 210
Hummingbird Heaven: 47
Institute for Field Ornithology/C.D. Duncan: 10 top, 233, 236
International Crane Foundation: 69 bottom
Jason Discovery: 23 center
Kachemak Bay Wilderness Lodge/M. McBride: 125 top bottom, 126, 128, 129
Kenai Fjords National Park: 124
James Landenberger: 109
Lenox Collections: 116 bottom, 117 bottom, 119 top
Lepp and Associates: 16 top, 32, 33
Leupold and Stevens, Inc.: 20 bottom right
Library of Congress: 78 top and bottom, 79 top and bottom, 80 all
Long Point Bird Observatory: 232, 237
Looker Products: 36 bottom
Mammoth Cave National Park: 163 top and bottom
Manitoba Tourism: 5 bottom, 131, 133 top and bottom, 134
Manomet Bird Observatory: 239
Marlab Specialities ProHarness: 27 right
Maslowski Wildlife Productions: 57
Mill Pond Press: 99, 100, 105, 106, 107
Mountaintop: 111 top
Mountain View Press: 112 bottom
National Audubon Society: 64 top and bottom, 65 all, 66, 67
National Wild Turkey Federation: 71, 72 bottom
The Nature Conservancy: 81 bottom
Nature House, Inc./Trio: 58, 59
New Zealand Tourist and Publicity Office: 224, 225 top and bottom, 226
North American Bluebird Society: 76
Padre Island National Seashore: 4 bottom, 8 top right, 72 top, 141 bottom, 142 top and bottom, 143, 144, 149, 156, 157 bottom
Flip Pallot: 10 bottom, 11, 146, 150 top, 153 top
Pictured Rocks National Lakeshore: 9 top
Point Reyes Bird Observatory: 235, 243
Point Reyes National Seashore: 135
Vern Wayne Pond: 115 top
Presto Galaxy: 37, back cover (hardcover)
Redwood National Park: 136 bottom, 137

Ruffed Grouse Society: 77 top and bottom
Shelburne Museum: 94
Sid Bell Originals: 115 bottom
Sigma Corporation of America: 25 (1, 2, 4, 5)
Silver Creek Industries: 28, 29
Skyflight Mobiles: 110
Society Expeditions: 12 top and bottom, 186, 188
Songscope: 22 bottom
J.D. Sprankle: 93
Steiner Prints: 92 top and bottom
Steuben Glass: 120 all, 121
St. Martin Tourist Office/John Forte: 191
Swarovski Optik: 20 bottom left, 22 top, 23 top
Swift Instruments Inc.: 18 top, 20 top
Tamrac: 16 bottom, 27 top left, 30 all, 31
The Thimbleberry: 111 bottom
Titan Art Glass: 95
Tokina Optical Corporation: 24 (2, 6, 7, 8)
Tourism, Recreation & Heritage New Brunswick: 5 top, 13 bottom, 130, 168 bottom
United States Government Bird Banding Laboratory: 234 top and bottom
USF&G: 15
Michael Van Houzen: 112 top
Vermont Comfort Birds: 114
VIREO: 176 bottom; 177; P. Alder, 178 bottom, 179; R. Behrstock, 173; O. Bill, 220; H. Brokaw, 172; C.H. Breenewalt, 175 bottom, 195, 198, 223, 229; R. Cartwell, 197 bottom; H. Cruickshank, 200, 201; K. Davey, 206; T.H. Dick, 199; J. Dunning, 174, 175 top, 176 top, 178 top; M. Groid, 216; M.P. Kahl, 196 top, 205, 209, 221, 222, 227; A. Mack, 217; C. Speeble, 214 bottom; D.&M. Zimmerman, 207
Visuals: 85
Vivitar Corporation: 19, 25 (3)
Voyageur Art, Inc.: 101, 109
Whitefish Point Bird Observatory: 240, 241, 244, 245 top
White Swan Ltd.: 53 top and bottom
Wildlife Products: 41
Yukon Tourism: 127